MOVING IN

Tales of an Unlicensed Marriage

Bruce Littlefield

Patrick + Ann—
Here's to love and laughs.
Thanks for being wonderful
people. Happy to know you.
June 2013 ♡ Bruce

ISBN: 1-4800-5081-4
ISBN-13: 978-1-4800-5081-5

"I first learned the concepts of
non-violence in my marriage."
--Ghandi

For Scott

Now can we renovate the house?

CONTENTS

FOREWORD (LOOKING BACK)

It was love at first sight. Okay, it was lust. But it was most definitely at first sight.

I was his first. And he, well, wasn't mine.

His girlfriend at the time had called to say she wanted me to meet someone. Her boyfriend!

As the story goes, when Scott started dating Deb (a really good catch after years of recreational catch and release) he told her that he might possibly be, "well, um, guh, guh, guh,… attracted to guys."

"You're great," she promptly said. "So, let's date awhile and see." Looking back on it now, Deb is quick to admit what she was really thinking—*this hunk is HOT and he's also nice. Definite marriage material. Please God, don't let him be guh, guh, guh,… attracted to guys.*

Eight months and a long line of sex specialists later—a quack psychiatrist, a female rabbi, a spiritual healer, and a well-recommended psychic—it was decided that Scott was positively, unequivocally, absolutely guh, guh, going to need to wave his big rainbow flag. Nothing and no one was ever going to change that. So the couple packed their bags and went on an un-honeymoon to St. Martin where they cracked open a couple bottles of champagne and celebrated their eight-month journey to enlightenment and their commitment to a lifelong friendship.

On the return flight home, Deb announced, "I have a friend I want you to meet."

That friend was me.

When Scott walked into the restaurant where I was working for our prearranged meeting, I remember my eyeballs wiggling in their sockets. I put down the candlestick I was polishing and whispered to my fellow waiter, "That's my friend Deb's ex. Soon to be known as 'my new husband.'"

Scott says he remembers seeing me walk down the staircase clad in my elegant tuxedo and instantly knew that I was the one. We said "hello" and never said goodbye.

That was twenty years ago.

There are a few stories in between lust at first sight and our decision to buy a house—a stint living with five other people in a tiny rent stabilized New York City apartment, working together as waiters, completing graduate studies, navigating the choppy waters of telling our families, and couples therapy—but those I'll save for another book. This is the one about how Scott and

I bought a house in the country and went about making it our home.

The story of the two boys who bought the old Hunt place starts like this—

1

MOVING DAY

"Twenty-six Footer." The U-Haul rental agent's words echoed in my mind like a bad Billy Ray Cyrus song as I squeezed my way up the capillary of a road called the Henry Hudson Parkway that winds up Manhattan's Westside. The road runs due north along the Hudson River and is the way out of the congested cacophony of New York City and up to the green serenity waiting on the other side of the Tappan Zee Bridge.

I was headed to the Catskills to close on the old farmhouse Scott and I had seen on the Esopus Creek. It was my third visit to the area. The first was the quick "we'll take it," and the second was for the home inspection, during which we had learned that the roof had "two to five years," the well was "filled with sulfur," and most of the electric wasn't "up to code." Undeterred, we signed the contract and were on our third trip up for the big closing. This time I had a sofa, loveseat, and ottoman rumbling along behind me in 1,538 cubic feet of cavernous U-Haul space.

I was in the driver's seat of a twenty-six foot storage unit on wheels, Jasper panting by my side and Scott following along behind in my 1984 red Fiero. I was in the monster because a) Scott's not a very good driver and b) the ten-foot mini mover, which I had reserved, was not available. "Rights now," U-Haul Mama had informed me that morning, "wees only gots the twenty-six foot Super Mover." When I tried to explain I was only moving one sofa, a loveseat, and an ottoman, and didn't really need all that space, the long, decorated nail of her forefinger pointed to the small print of the rental agreement, which clearly stated substitutions were possible. What I had before me was a take it or leave it situation, and I could hear the line of New Yorkers behind me huffing like a pack of dingoes looking to take down a baby. "Alright," I said, agreeing to drive the hippopotamus of U-Hauls. "As long as I get it for the price I was quoted."

"I ain't got no problem with that," she told me, pointing her nail to the bottom of the paperwork. "Sign here."

After packing the sofa, ottoman and loveseat, I had pulled away from our walk-up apartment, turned right on 96th Street and gotten on the Parkway. The road was a tight squeeze. My eyes were therefore concentrating on attempting to stay in my lane and not wandering around looking for "No Trucks Allowed" signs.

Twenty-six Footer had power steering, air conditioning, and more mirrors than a beauty contest, but I would disagree with the U-Haul agent's promise that it was "the truck that drives like a van." In fact, so would the law. I was about to discover that state troopers felt that if it drives like a van but looks like a truck, it's a truck.

The whirl of sirens pulled me over to a tire-screeching stop. Given Code Blue's mad dash out of his police car, I was sure he thought I was heading to blow apart the Tappan Zee. Or, a more gruesome thought—maybe I had accidentally bumped the orange-clad highwayman I had passed a hundred or so yards back. He had been waving his flag rather dramatically.

I rolled down the window and flashed my most pitiful I-swear-I-wasn't-speeding look. He glared up at me and yelled, "What, are you crazy? You can't drive a truck on the Henry Hudson Parkway!"

"It was supposed to be a van," I said meekly. Jasper jumped on my lap, panting and hoping this guy had a treat. "If it's not a van, what should I do?"

"GET IT OFF!" At least he was clear. With flight attendant arm movements, Officer Blue with the bushy eyebrows instructed me to turn my illegal twenty-six foot beast around at the toll plaza and take the George Washington Bridge out of town.

During my near arrest, I had caught a glimpse of Scott in one of the many mirrors of the truck. He was sitting sheepishly in my little red sports car in the emergency lane a few hundred feet back. After maneuvering twenty-six feet of truck through the toll plaza and paying the toll in *both* directions, I picked up my cell phone and called Scott. "Don't get mad at me," he said, anticipating my fury. "It's not my fault!"

"I'll blame later!" I screeched. "Just figure out how to get us to the George Washington Bridge." *End call.*

Little Red zipped around me and headed south toward the majestic suspension bridge in the distance. *Somehow, it is your fault*, I seethed inside. Then, I reminded myself to take a deep breath. *We're going to the country to get away from stress.* I turned up the a/c and called Scott back. "Do you know how to get there?" I asked nicely, swallowing a passive aggressive edge.

"Yes." *End call.*

From my nosebleed vantage point atop the Hippo, I could see the green sign in the distance—"George Washington Bridge, right lane." At last, good-bye city life, hello country.... Then, the unbelievable: Little Red gets in the *left* lane. *The right lane!* I scream. Jasper pops up and looks around. For a moment, I thought of letting Little Red drive on and living happily ever after somewhere else. After all, I had the sofa set. But Little Red had the $42,000 in certified checks. Follow that car!

Within ten seconds of seeing the call to glory—George Washington Bridge, right lane—we were again headed north on the Henry Hudson Parkway back towards Mr. Blue and his bushy-brows. I hit redial.

"You idiot!" I road raged. *End call.*

I floored Twenty-six Footer and, in a theatrical move into the emergency lane, I overtook Little Red, but in my effort to avoid Bushy Brow and the Orange Highwaymen, I exited into an area of the city I had never seen, and hope to never see again. After a three-point turn, a brief wrong way stint on a one-way street, and a close call with a startled squirrel, Twenty-six Footer found its way to the George Washington Bridge, shadowed annoyingly by Little Red.

A mad fight via cell phones broke out between the occupants of the two vehicles. With views as opposite as the sizes of our transports, the fight would last the entire way to the Garden State Parkway. It went something like this:

"Say you're sorry." *End call.* "I'm not sorry." *End call.* "Yes, you are." *End call.* "I'm pulling over if you don't apologize." *End call.* "Pull over. I don't care." *End call.* "I'm pulling over." *End call.* "Pull over." *End call.* "I'm really pulling over."

Well, actually, I'm slowing down so I'll be out of your sight and you'll think I've pulled over.

Very slowly I crawled along the highway until finally my cell phone rang. "Where are you?"

"I pulled over until you apologize," I said, not sure why I'm owed an apology.

"Apologize! For what?"

"For making me drive this overblown box on wheels!" When pressured I can think quickly.

"I'll drive it," he answered.

"You'll wreck it. You're a *horrible* driver." *End call.* Not quite a conversation, but it was more than one sentence. We were getting somewhere.

Meanwhile, as I crept along at the state minimum, I was passed by drivers either shaking their fists and blowing their horns or giving me "I've-moved-too" pity looks. My phone rang again after what seems like an hour, but was probably only after a mile or two.

"This is supposed to be the greatest day of our lives," Scott implored. "Where are you?"

"Way back," I said, proudly indignant.

"Meet me at the first gas station on the Parkway."

"Okay." *End call.*

I pulled into the Exxon. Scott was nowhere in sight. "Where are you?" I demanded via cell phone.

"At the first gas station."

"No, you're not," I said. "I am." *End call.*

My phone rang again. "Okay, meet me at the second gas station."

Distracted with my cell phone call antics, I clipped the tollbooth with one of Twenty-six Footer's many mirrors. "Watch it guy!" the attendant said, stumbling backwards.

"Sorry, it's moving day," was all I could muster.

I now issue a blanket apology to all those at the second gas station on the Garden State Parkway who witnessed a man in a U-Haul lose it.

"You're right," Scott said after I climaxed my performance with an instructional display of the dizzying multi-mirrored kaleidoscope that showed every glaring metal angle above, around and under the monster. "It's like a bad amusement park ride in here." I accepted his apology, even though he failed to mention the right lane/left lane fiasco, and we made nice. We had more important business to get to. We were off to the country to close on a house, Little Red followed by Twenty-six Footer.

2

WE'LL TAKE IT

How we ended up purchasing a house in the country began as one big and miraculous mistake.

On a quick weekend escape from New York's stress, we had taken a trip with friends to New Hope. They excitedly spoke of a house they had just seen in Rosendale, New York—a converted barn with two ponds, beautiful views, and surrounded by lots of creative types. "Cool," I asked. "But where's Rosendale?"

"Near New Paltz," Bonnie explained. I had been trapped in the city for a few years too long. Directions to anywhere in my life could be boiled down to "around the corner from Pottery Barn" or "across from the Starbucks."

"New Paltz is where we had our wedding," Rob explained. Their wedding had been one of those perfect days at an old mountaintop hotel. "Oh, the Mohawk House!" I said. "It's gorgeous up there."

"Mo*honk*," Bonnie corrected. I had thought during their wedding it was odd to name an elegant 19th century castle after a Native American hairstyle, and now I stood corrected.

So, we spent our weekend with Bonnie and Rob at a small purple bed and breakfast in New Hope, mostly listening to them enthuse about the perfect place they were going to buy. *A place in the country*, I oohed and aahed to myself, *how wonderful that would be!*

We returned to the city on Sunday, and on a whim, I decided to give myself an hour of daydreaming. I searched "homes for sale in Rosendale." Then, neighboring High Falls. Scott joined me at my desk, as did Jasper. We quickly found a cute house by a waterfall in Minnewaska for $110,000. "Let's call!" I said, never before even thinking of buying a house.

Scott looked at the excited determination in my eyes and, perhaps to avoid an argument, impulsively agreed. Scott, a top real estate agent in Manhattan, might have also been happy to waste another realtor's time besides his own.

We made an appointment with an eccentric agent named Raiza to go up on Saturday, do some hiking and see the house. I could hardly wait! I love to shop and had already concluded that house shopping was the Olympics of all shopping.

We got the tragic call on Monday.

"Brucie, Scotty. Raiza here!" announced the Moroccan-Israeli accent on our answering machine. "Terrible, terrible news. Your little house went into foreclosure and dropped $25,000 in price. It has an accepted offer." I was instantly heartsick and suddenly cutthroat. "Let's outbid them!" I schemed, only to learn that in the country real estate sales don't work quite like they do in the city. We would have to wait to see if that deal fell through. Raiza explained, "You vill have to vait to see if dat sale falls through and come see it Saturday as a backup."

Saturday couldn't come quick enough. I begged Raiza, "Let's make it this Thursday instead."

On Thursday morning Scott took a day off from his clients and showings. I postponed a book deadline, and we loaded Jasper—yes, our furry son would have to like it too—into a rental car and took off for the unknown. Two hours later, we were shaking hands with a large woman in overalls who was about to change our life.

"I want to take you to a special house first," Raiza said and told us the price. "I know it's a little more d'an you want to spend, but…" *A little more than a little more*, I thought, but we played along as we had no real intention of actually *buying* any house anyway. We might as well see what the area had to offer.

"No harm looking," Scott said. Infamous last words.

As we turned onto Hurley Mountain Road and peeked over the railing of the weathered bridge, we could see a babbling creek. Perched high above it stood a glorious slate blue farmhouse. The gravel crunched beneath our tires, and my heart pounded in my chest. We followed Raiza down the winding drive past a small cottage on stilts jutting out over the water.

"Boy," Scott said, "that place needs some serious TLC."

"I know. Isn't it adorable?"

We walked into the welcoming grace of a 1920's farmhouse. I could feel past good times bouncing off the walls. We scanned the listing Raiza handed us: "Year built, 1924. Square footage, 2400. Bedrooms, four. Water features, creek frontage/Class A trout stream. Notes: Former Edgewater Farm bungalow colony."

Scott and I surveyed the big living room and gave each other a quick "don't-get-excited" look, followed by a silent "get-the-price-down" nod. I doggedly searched for something to bring the price down on the house we weren't going to buy.

We looked in the kitchen—a wonderful antique coal stove. We looked in the master bedroom—a ten-foot paned window overlooking a peach tree and a claw foot tub in the bathroom. I found in the upstairs loft what was sure to knock thousands off the asking price. "Ewwwww!" I said, pointing to the critters crawling up onto the round window. "Look at all those bugs."

"D'ose are ladybugs!" Raiza said. "D'ey're very good luck."

"Even the bugs are perfect," I mumbled to Scott. We acted only mildly interested, except for Jasper who was already posing picture perfect in front of the giant window in the living room. "Well," I told Raiza, "let's see the other place."

In the privacy of our car driving towards the Internet foreclosure by the waterfall, Scott and I couldn't stop talking. *We aren't here to buy! We're just looking.* It was the first house we had seen, *ever,* and even two city boys could tell the house had structural problems. Surely something bad. *Anything*! *We couldn't actually buy a house*!

Then, we drove down the long, muddy, where-in-the-heck-are-we-going driveway to the Internet house, the one that started this whole pipe dream. It did indeed have a waterfall on the property! But it also had 1970's orange Formica cabinets, a too skinny spiral staircase, and a roof that sagged worse than Phyllis

Diller's butt. When we tossed a rock underneath the darkened basement, we heard a tsunami-sized splash.

We got in our car and couldn't back down the muddy driveway fast enough. Congratulations foreclosure buyers! May I suggest turning your basement into a koi pond?

"Please take us back," we begged. We had to get back to Hurley Mountain Road before someone else did! Suddenly, we *had* to have that house. We had no idea where we were on the map, but we didn't care.

Raiza happily humored us as we turned on every faucet, banged on every wall, and flushed every toilet. Then, in a move of real real estate agent chutzpah, Raiza locked the door, told us to spend time walking around the property, and left. We stood on the old wooden porch. We admired the daffodils just beginning to poke their arms from the wet earth, watched old Jasper frolic like a pup in the yard, and listened to the gurgling of the sparkling Esopus Creek.

"What just happened?" I asked, taking Scott's hand.

"I'm not quite sure," Scott said, stupefied. "I think we just bought a house."

3

HOW TO SET A TRAP

The day we closed on our house—the very same day of the U-Haul fiasco—we unloaded our sofa, carried it into the living room, and collapsed atop its plastic-wrapped cushions. I looked out the big picture window to the lawn.

"The grass is a little higher than I remember. Guess that'll have to be cut soon."

"Let's just take a minute," Scott said wisely, "and appreciate that we made it." So, we closed our eyes in thanks for what was soon to be a lifelong project, and welcomed the calm with a deep breath.

"You smell that?" I asked, my moment of relaxation and gratefulness interrupted by an odor unlike any I had ever smelled in the city.

"Not me. I swear!" Scott answered defensively.

An all out odor hunt ensued. It wasn't Jasper, though he could have used a "B-A-T-H." It wasn't the water, though it smelled "like rotten eggs." It wasn't the refrigerator, though there was "something growing in the dairy drawer!" No, it was a *different* smell, and it was coming from the oldest part of the house—the wing that was once the kitchen when the property was a bungalow colony known as "Edgewater Farm." We heard the culprit scratching around below the room that was to be my office. A skunk had set up shop beneath the floor. After a day of U-Hauling and check writing, we decided we could hold our noses and live in peace with Pepe Le Pew for a day or two. "We will think of him as our first house guest," I sentimentalized in a pinched nose nasal. "Just close the door." We went back to our couch to watch our grass grow.

"I guess we should call someone," I said.

"For the skunk?" Scott asked.

"No. The grass," I said. I'd actually forgotten from too many years of city life that grass actually did grow. "I swear it's gotten higher in the last five minutes."

In the kitchen I found the business cards of several gardeners, along with some from electricians, plumbers, contractors, roofers, and a Feng Shui expert. "Maybe I better save these," I said with growing homeowner awareness. "Just in case." I picked the pretty card of *Immy and Jim Casey's Garden and Hearth.* I liked the slogan—*We make your home easy to live in and love.* I figured that was what we wanted to do.

After realizing our cell phones got no reception, I pessimistically lifted the receiver, hoping whatever-the-Ma-Bell-it-is had turned on our phone. "Dial tone!" I proudly called out to Scott who was still sitting with Jasper on the couch. I dialed my first call from the real live country! I smiled at the comforting hum of Ma Bell.

"You-do-not-need-to-dial-the-area-code-before-dialing-this-number," the automated voice admonished. "Please-hang-up-and-try-your-call-again." My following dial got a sweet woman's voice. "Oh, I'm so glad you called us," she said. "That house is very special. We were the caretakers there for a couple of years. Did the owner give you our name?"

He hadn't. I just liked the promising look of the ivy growing up the "C" of "Casey" on their card. We decided she'd come by bright and early the next morning.

"Well?" Scott asked as I came back into the living room.

"She's coming by tomorrow to talk to us about our gardens," I said happily.

"Our what?" Scott asked.

"Our gardens," I said with authority.

"I just want the grass cut," Scott said. He could see that we were about to chop more green than just grass.

The following morning—after my night of dreaming about our gardens—Jasper greeted Immy's big blue pick-up with a country "And who are youuuuuuu," howl. She climbed out of the pick-up wearing a sundress, a perfectly weathered straw hat, and a million-dollar smile. We walked around to the back of the house and Immy's blue eyes widened. "It's high!" she said as she parted the tall glades. "I guess we could cut it the first time and see what we've got."

"And then what?" I asked sheepishly. My only experience with a patch of green in the city was our Astroturf doormat.

"I know someone," Immy said.

I scrawled in my notebook as she talked: Delphiniums! Lavender mist! Stargazer lilies, forsythia, umbrella pine, compost.... "You don't need to write it down," she laughed. "That's what you've got me for."

"What exactly are you suggesting we do?" Scott blurted out at one point. Immy and I turned around to look at him. "I mean, exactly how much is this going to cost?"

"Watch out!" Immy said, as she grabbed Scott's arm. "Poison ivy!" We all looked up at a tree crawling with poison ivy and then over to a fence covered in poison ivy. I instantly started scratching. And then, Immy pointed as Jasper traipsed out of a *meadow* of poison ivy.

"If your dog rubs up against you," Immy warned, "you'll get it."

So, money suddenly became no object. In fear of saying hello to red rashes, we prepared to say goodbye to our greenbacks. "What can you do about Jasper?" I begged.

Immy took command. "First, we cover ourselves in this white powder called Ivy Coat. Then, after spraying everything with ivy killer, we wash off with a lotion called Tecnu—I have plenty of it in the truck—just in case we came in contact with any of it. Next week, we'll spray again. Then, wait a week. Till..."

My head was spinning as much as my leg was itching. "How long will it take before we can plant something harmless?"

"A week, a month, maybe two," Immy said. "But after the soil is ready, we'll go shopping for plants."

"How much?" Scott asked.

"A few hundred dollars," she said to both our relief. I thought that sounded very reasonable for such a necessary work. "We only charge for our time."

I realized Immy could have charged us anything. "Do our gardens then!" I said. "We have to be able to pet Jasper."

The next day Immy and her ruggedly handsome husband Jim came over in the rain to set a trap with a very long rope to catch the skunk Pepe. "I don't want to hurt it," I told Jim as he set a trap with marshmallows and a curled up piece of pizza. "It won't kill him, will it?"

"Well, it's going to raise its cholesterol," Jim chuckled.

"And what are we going to do with it once we catch it?"

"We'll drag it to the woods and let it go," he explained.

The following morning Scott and I peeked around the corner of our house and noticed that the trap had been emptied of marshmallows and pizza but had moved and was sitting beneath a bushy dark tree.

"That's weird," I puzzled. "Why didn't the trap work? And who moved the trap?"

Within the hour, my two ivy-killers cum skunk-hunters once again rolled down our driveway in their big blue truck. "...And when we found it," I said, concluding the empty trap tale, "it was right over there beneath that big tree with nothing in it!"

"Yew," Immy said.

"No, it."

"No," she said, pointing. "That's not a tree, that's a yew."

"Yeah, over there by you."

"Yew," Immy answered. "It's a shrub. But that is weird that there's no skunk."

"That's exactly what I said," I told her.

So, we reset the trap, once again with marshmallows minus the stale pizza, and substituted graham crackers. "With a little chocolate," I laughed, "the stinker could make S'mores."

Same scenario. Different day.

"...But this time," I explained in a call to Immy. "The trap was by the backdoor! It was like the skunk was going to drag it back to the house with him."

"Well that's the darnedest thing I've ever heard!"

Once again we set the trap and decided to take turns watching it from an upstairs window. I hadn't been there more than three minutes when I witnessed the crime that was about to unfold. Jasper walked up to the trap, took the rope in his mouth, and shook the cage silly as if he was conquering a wild animal. And one by one he devoured the marshmallows that plopped out like candy from his personal piñata.

"JASPER! You dirty dog!" I screamed from behind the window. He ignored my muted screams and finished his sweet treat.

Jasper's fat count was climbing higher than our poison ivy, so we decided to give it a break and not evict Pepe just yet. Perhaps, we reasoned, if we let the skunk squat for a few weeks, he'd get tired of us and decide to move on.

"Besides," I declared, delicately closing the door to what would someday be a great office, "we're not going to get to that renovation for at least a month."

4

THE JACUZZI CULTURE

We returned the U-Haul to the neighboring metropolis of Kingston (New York's first state capital), and we stopped by Home Depot to "pick up a few things." While Scott grabbed a practical toilet plunger, I ogled the Jacuzzi selection.

"Nope," Scott said firmly, pointing the plunger forward. "Keep walking."

"It's only $2500!" I whined, a bit too loudly. "This is a great deal. "Everywhere else they're at least $6000."

"And how would *you* know?"

"I did a little research online."

"Well, we are *not* buying a Jacuzzi," Scott said, with added emphasis on the *not*. "We just bought a house!"

"I'm sorry, but I'm buying it," I said. "I know a good deal when I see one."

"Don't you dare!" he threatened.

We now had an eager audience of an orange vested Homer and a Nosy Nancy cradling a puffy toilet seat in her arms.

"Besides, when you add the extras like the electric and a cement pad," Scott argued, "$2500 becomes $6000 very quickly."

I turned to Homer. "What do you think?" I asked.

"I think I don't want to be involved," he said adjusting his badly askew toupee.

"He doesn't want to be involved," I said turning to Scott, "because he is too much of a gentleman to tell you you're wrong. But he knows it's a good deal. Right?" I smiled at Nancy and nodded at Homer. "We all agree."

With that, I confidently pulled out my credit card and did the dirty deed.

When we got home, Jim and Immy were standing in the middle of the poison ivy patch dressed in the garden version of radioactive fall-out suits. Their faces were painted white like drunken circus clowns. They were much more excited about the idea of our Jacuzzi than Scott had been and agreed they would enjoy coming over for a soak. "Terrific!" Immy enthused. "We'll plan some impressive landscaping around it."

"See, Scott," I chided. "Everybody loves it, and you'll learn to love it too."

"By the way I want you to meet my son on Saturday night." Immy said in her white face. She tossed her trowel into the wheelbarrow. "So, you're invited to a dinner party at the home of David and Adam at 7 o'clock. We do their gardens too! They're best friends of my son, Ben, and his best friend, Hector."

When Jim and Immy backed their truck out of our driveway, I turned to Scott and asked, "What does that dinner party sound like to you?"

"Um," he guessed. "Fun?"

He obviously didn't see the yellow brick billboard. "Except for Immy," I said, "it sounds like *all men*."

"Oh!" he said, finally getting it. I hoped.

Off to our first dinner party in the country.

When Saturday came, we dressed in city-to-country casual, packed a bottle of wine in an old wire basket, and climbed into our tiny two-seater and headed to our first country dinner party. The cornstalks stood at attention along the sides of the road. They, like the rest of us, were waiting for rain. It was the summer we would all wait for rain.

We were taking in the scenery and B.B. King was jazzing from the car stereo when I noticed a hand-lettered "Eggs for Sale" sign. "How do we know if those eggs are okay to eat?" I asked, remembering something my mother had said one time about some eggs being fertilized and some not and wondered if there might be baby chicks tucked inside.

"Farmers just know," Scott said assuredly. "Farmers always know."

Farmers, I thought, *usually live in farmhouses with a barn. That guy lives in a trailer with a cage full of chickens.* How could I know I won't be lighting the stove tomorrow morning, spraying the Pam, and cracking open a baby chicken? I was pondering this thought with the seriousness of the *Which Came First* debate, when Scott slammed on the brakes. Our car screeched, swerved, and skidded, and I braced for head-on impact.

We came to a whiplash stop. Thankfully, a bashed Bambi was nowhere in sight. The seatbelt had left its pattern on my shirt, but everything on my body felt in its proper place.

Scott pointed at a dark patch in the middle of the road. It was moving, slowly. "What is that?" I whispered.

"I think it's a… turtle?" Scott leapt out of the car and into action. Jumping in front of an approaching Volvo, he heroically thrusted his arm in the air to stop it before it flattened the slow walker. With arm raised, he stood there in his suspendered khakis and white linen shirt, watching the turtle slowly make its way to the grassy finish line. The two beautiful girls in the parked Volvo watched him airlift the turtle and carry it into the woods, sending it on its way with a happy pat. The entire scene looked like a live-action Banana Republic ad.

The two Volvo girls applauded and I beamed proudly, loving this new country version of Scott. Scott then made a manly victory jaunt back towards the car until his leather-soled sandals slipped on the pavement and, in one ungracious spasm, he toppled onto his butt with legs in the air and arms flailing. For a moment our fable's hero squirmed in the middle of the road like an overturned turtle himself. Once righted, he crawled into the car.

"Do you think they saw me?" Scott sheepishly asked just as the Volvo came around us. The girls were pointing and laughing hysterically.

"Yep," I said. "They definitely saw you."

The turtle episode made us what we call in the city, "fashionably late." But in the country it's known as "country time." Scott was also fashionably soiled. But in the country, it's called, well, "dirty."

After a glass of wine or vodka, depending on what your liver needs, we toured our hosts' gardens. I couldn't remember which one was "David" and which was "Adam," but together they had a variety of beautiful gardens, each with a different theme. As we walked around they announced the name of each garden. There was a "Shakespeare Garden," filled with the plants mentioned by the Bard himself. There was the "Blue Garden," filled with, well, blue flowers. There was the all-white "Serenity Garden," furthest from the road. And, of course, there was the requisite vegetable garden, cleverly coined with signage: "The Garden of Eatin'."

"And last..." the more full-figured of our two hosts announced as Immy joined the end of our tour, "This one here is our moonlight garden."

"Only plants that twinkle in the moonlight," Immy added proudly.

"It's incredible," I said. "How much of this was here when you bought the house?"

"When we moved in," the taller, skinnier host said, "the whole yard was filled with basically weeds."

"Weeds and poison ivy," Immy reminded them.

I looked at Scott and knew exactly what he was thinking. His eyes were screaming, *These gardens cost more than a few hundred dollars, and I will be putting my foot down as soon as we're alone!!!*

Over dinner, we learned that Jim and Immy had been dairy farmers in Minnesota, and migrated east when Reagan pulled out the farm subsidies causing local farmers to go bankrupt.

During dessert, I learned how to castrate a bull. "A rubber band will do the trick," Jim explained over one too many glasses of wine. "Yep. You take a rubber band and wrap it tightly around the bull's you-know-what's and then wait..."

"Ouch," I squirmed in my seat, my groin tingling. "That's so mean."

"Nah," he said. "It's much better than cutting. The rubber band just constricts the blood flow. So, in no time, the you-know-what's just fall right off."

The following weekend we were invited to Woodstock for a musical production of *Imaginary Invalid.* Raiza, our real estate agent, was the director. (As we would discover, everyone in the country does more than one thing.) We joined a group of people going to dinner before the show, and I found myself in a lengthy conversation with a Ruth Buzzi look-alike about her son's failed potty training.

"When he sits on his potty, I sit on mine," she explained with motherly love. "And of course I can't laugh, even when he scrunches the face." With a constipated squint, she demonstrated for our table his determined, concentrated "I'm going-to-get-the-job done" face.

"You should write these things down," I chuckled. "I've always said God gave mothers a special gift for dealing with things others can't—like potty training, cleaning up vomit, and finessing all of life's *delicate* situations!"

"That's easy," she continued. "But how should a mother explain to her son when he gets excited?"

"What do you mean *excited?*" I asked naively.

She pointed…*"down there"*… and repeated, slowly, "Ex-cite-ed."

I took out my notebook, to disguise my uncomfortable fidget. "I don't really know," I offered. "No one ever explained it to me."

It turned out the Ruth Buzzi mom had a "subscription to every baby-faced magazine and a bookshelf of parenting books." And according to her, you're supposed to say: "It's normal, honey." Or "It's okay." My personal favorite is: "Don't worry, it will go away."

A woman with a big bush of red hair interrupted our conversation. "Have either of you ever read the book *A Tale of Two Titties?*" I shook my head and wondered if there was something in the country water that made people spill all their stuff.

"Well," she continued, lifting her jaw almost boastfully, "*I* drew the cover! I'd invite you over to my house to see my work, of course, but I don't know where I live!"

She laughed, waiting for someone to take the bait.

"So, why don't you know where you live?" I asked.

"Because I don't have an address yet," she complained. It turned out she too was a "weekender" and this was when I realized everyone around the table was a client of Raiza. She explained that Raiza had recently sold her a house on Route 209, "But it didn't come with a mailbox! So, when I have someone over, I have to stand in front of my house waiting and waving." She explained that she had even walked up and down the busy highway, dodging traffic, on a mission to find out the addresses her neighbors claimed. None of the numbers made sense, she concluded and had finally decided, "This weekend I'm just going to make one up. Maybe you'll come and visit"

"Are you a writer?" a baldheaded fellow asked as I feverishly scribbled in my notebook.

"Yes, that's right. But don't hold it against me."

"I am, too," he said. "But it's been slow for me, so I moonlight writing porn for *Inches* magazine." Was this whole dinner a practical joke? I looked down at my glass of water, then back up at the bald guy, and decided I better switch to wine. "My first piece is out this month," he bragged.

"So, what's it about?" I asked.

"Sex."

"That's obvious. I mean the story-line." He explained that the "scenario" involves a "studly" law enforcement officer and a New York City ordinance against throwing away your junk mail in public trashcans. "Anyway, the cop shows up at an apartment on 103rd Street to issue a ticket…"

"Is that really a law?" I interrupted.

"Yeah. Can you believe it?"

I couldn't. But as soon as I got home I rushed to the computer to learn that according to section 16-120E of New York City's Health and Administration Code, it is indeed illegal to throw any household trash in a public garbage can. I also confirmed that "A Tale of Two Titties" is a very popular title.

"Bruce! Scott!" Raiza yelled to us after *Imaginary Invalid*, which was not worth mentioning. "How *deed* you like dee show?"

"What a show!" I answered diplomatically, while stepping on Scott's foot. He kept his mouth shut, but nodded enthusiastically.

"I vant you to meet my friend Valerie," Raiza said, yanking a woman in a sparkly blue blouse out of a conversation she was having. "Vell, Val, dese are my new friends, Bruce and Scott. Dey are dee newest members of dee 'Jacooozzi Culture.'"

"But how'd you know that, Raiza?"

"Know vat?"

"About the Jacuzzi."

"Dat's what we call de weekenders. Every one of dem buy a house and den dey buy a Jacooozzi."

"Ours is coming next week," I admitted, feeling uncharacteristically embarrassed.

"See dat?" Raiza said to Val.

Poor Val was cringing. "Don't worry," I said, laughing at our new moniker. "It'll just give me something to write about."

Val laughed with relief. "Oh, you're a writer? You should check out the *Blue Star Press*. It's a great local paper."

"I'd love to. Where do I get it?"

"Oh, most anywhere. Emmanuel's has it."

"Emmanuel's?" I asked.

"The grocery store," she explained.

The following morning I made my first visit to Emmanuel's Marketplace, a local store that's clean, well stocked, and equally priced to city standards. I asked the cashier where the *Blue Star* was.

"You mean the ointment?" she asked.

"No, *The Blue Star* paper."

"You must mean the *Blue Stone*," she said, laughing out loud. "The *Blue Stone's* the paper, and the Blue Star's a jock itch cream." She pointed to the front counter where I could see a stack of newspapers. As I slunk over to grab a copy, she continued laughing and yelled out after me, "I thought you mighta had a fungus."

5

HOW TO DRAIN A POND

"Hello?" a woman's nasal voice answered at *The Blue Stone Press*.

"May I speak to the editor?"

"This is *her*."

I momentarily debated whether the incorrect grammar was a test. "Oh hi," I said. "I'm calling about your 'Writer Wanted' ad in the paper…"

"Yeah," she said, cutting me off and quickly getting to the qualifications. "We're looking for someone full-time with a couple of years experience on a local paper."

"I couldn't do full-time," I explained. "I'm finishing a book on Hillary Clinton, but I was thinking about writing a column about buying a country house."

"Write three," she instructed like a countrified Anna Wintour. "And then we'll talk."

According to the editor, my columns made her laugh, "at times hysterically." She said she'd publish the first three as submitted. And over the next few weeks, she ran the stories of our U-Haul drama, our poison ivy battle, and our Jacuzzi purchase. After three columns, she called to tell me that readers loved it and wanted more.

"Can you get me another one by tomorrow?" she asked. "People are really buying papers."

"Sure," I said. The interview with Hillary Clinton's college friend could wait. I had no idea I was about to be the star of small town drama.

Here's my fourth column as it ran:

MOVING IN

By Bruce Littlefield

I've discovered why Jabba the Hutt is taking a break from the *Star Wars* saga. Jabba is very busy with a new career—selling real estate in Ulster County. I met her Jabba-ness when she almost sold a house to my good friends. Actually, she almost sold them a *bog*—with a house floating in it.

The weekend after we moved into our house, our friends, whose wedding at the Mohonk House had prompted our return to the area and the spur-of-the-moment decision to buy a house, asked us to go see the converted barn in Rosendale that they were in the process of buying:

Open, airy, converted barn on 3 private acres.

2 swimming ponds and sunset deck. Mountain views.

The four of us, along with a contractor who had been giving us some hefty estimates on work to be done on our house, drove over to see what was soon to be their house. They had already signed a "binder" and written a deposit check, but wanted one more look and a second opinion. Jabba, the slovenly real estate agent with that recognizable figure, was salivating to make the deal. We were soon to discover that Jabba (whose identity I'm protecting not because she deserves it, but for the sake of any little Jabbas she has running around) was probably the only person in the county praying for the drought to continue.

We drove down the driveway towards the converted barn, passing a pond on the right, then a pond on the left. We parked, and I excitedly stepped out of the car. *Thluck. Thluck.* My new Nike's squished into mud. "Wow, the barn looks cool," I said trying to selflessly forget my soiled sneakers. From the other side of the car, I heard another round of *Thluck. Thluck.* "Yuck," Scott said, calling it as he stepped in it. "The pond must have overflowed." We all turned and looked toward the pond that sat nearly fifty feet away.

Jabba rolled out of her car. On her way over to greet us, the real estate agent dodged patches of mud as if she didn't notice they were there. "Did you notice the beautiful sculpture on the way in?" she asked, her legs strategically straddling a bubbling demi-stream. "It's really my favorite."

We were all introduced.

In retrospect, I may have heard Jabba release a small gasp when she found out that two of the unannounced people on this excursion were Scott, one of Manhattan's top realtors, and our soon-to-be contractor who had tagged along to give our friends an estimate on re-shingling the barn's pitched roof.

"They need to do something about the lawn," I said as we sloshed through the everglades toward the front door.

"Oh, they just haven't cut the grass in a while," Jabba explained. "And the tall grass is keeping in the moisture." *The county is in the middle of a devastating drought*, I thought to myself, *and she thinks the grass is holding in moisture? We are walking on water! Didn't anyone else notice?*

As Jabba fumbled with the realtor key box, the door opened. The current tenant was home. "We had an appointment," Jabba said with a begging smile.

"It's alright," the girl said, "you won't bother me." I was uncomfortable being in the house while the tenant who was renting it was there, and it soon became evident that Jabba was also uncomfortable with us being in the house while the tenant who was renting it was there.

We spread out to take in the surroundings. Jabba rushed room-to-room, in the house and out of the house, trying to keep all the conversations in check. Outside the backdoor, she found me dodging bees as they were zipping by like mad dive-bombers. "Don't move and they won't bother you," Jabba said as she unflinchingly allowed an errant bee to crawl across her face. "These are honey bees. Don't you like honey?"

"Yes," I said. "But I prefer it in jars."

I rushed inside to escape the bees and found our friends in serious conversation with the tenant. Jabba stayed outside, braving the bees, in order to monitor the conversation of two others in our expedition party: the city realtor and the country contractor. Inside the barn, our friends had the tenant talking. I walked in on the tail end of a "when I moved in… there was a furry creature living in the oven" conversation.

"It was either a squirrel or an opossum," Tenant confirmed. "And sometimes I still see droppings." Next, Tenant showed us a scientific demonstration of how incredibly slanted the floor was. She placed a coffee mug on one end of the wooden kitchen table. Jabba walked in as the mug slid to the other end.

"You can make the table level by putting some coasters or wood blocks under one side," the agent quickly said.

The contractor asked if he could check the plumbing. Jabba followed him into the bathroom, huffing and puffing from her vigorous efforts.

"The water is unpredictable," Tenant told us. She turned on the kitchen faucet and what dribbled out can only be described as mucus in a glass. "Well," she noted, as we each leaned in to smell the glass of mucky juice, "predictable." Fortunately for Jabba's health, she was still in the bathroom explaining to our contractor how easy it is to redo galvanized pipes. Had she been in the kitchen to witness this scene, she would have certainly chugged the glass of mucous, and even asked for seconds to prove its purity.

We all gave each other the we've-seen-enough nod and headed for the exit. *Any exit.* The house was not what they remembered. *It couldn't be.*

I walked out of the living room onto the deck. Jabba was there. "I saw the most beautiful sunset I have ever seen in my life from this deck," she said in one last desperate attempt. I couldn't say a word. I just hurriedly waded toward the car. It was our only lifeboat off this sinking ship.

Jabba cornered Scott as he was trying to get to the car. "How's it going?" she asked.

"Not good," he said, losing all subtlety. "Not good at all." Deciding it was time to be blunt—realtor to realtor—Scott let her know this deal, like the house, was probably all washed up. "The house is under water. And our friends are upset."

"I'm sure it's drainage," she reported as four car doors slammed in quick succession. Then, she yelled, "I know a great pond specialist!"

I rolled down the window and yelled, "You need a *dam* engineer!"

That night, as we sat around the first campfire at our house, we relived Jabba's tour de force and shared one of those big guffaw laughs we'll always remember. We celebrated our moving in while acknowledging their *movin' on*!

But if anyone wants a house where you can swim to your front door and study wildlife while cooking, I know where one is for sale. And, if the house has sold during the drought, I apologize to the new tenants for not getting this out sooner. But I do know someone that knows a great pond specialist.

6

HORROR-SCOPE

The house we bought wasn't without its own problems. The building inspection report that we ordered pursuant to our mortgage agreement, and then promptly ignored pursuant to our wallet, read like the Surgeon General's report on cigarettes. Rather than tackling the "aging roof," the "sulfur infused water," the "sagging kitchen floor," or the "cracked and dangerous windows," I had bought a hot tub. And then we chose cosmetic over structural. We decided our first real construction project would be to open up the ceiling in the living room, which would create cathedral ceilings and a two-story view of the creek.

A month into owning the house, we raced up the New York Thruway, eager to see the results of our *contractor's overpriced handiwork. While Jasper ran around outside (hot on the trail of* Le Pew, I assumed), we ran inside to admire our first aesthetic expenditure on the house.

"Oh. My. God!" I screamed from the top of the stairs.

"What is it?" Scott shouted as he bounded up the steps two at a time.

Our contractor had finished the railing surrounding the loft and, without consulting us, decided on a surprise colored stain. "YELLOW!" we yelled together.

Immy and Jim raced in fresh from the poison ivy field to find out what all the noise was about. "Oh," Immy said, making what would become her trademark *eeek* face. "That's very yellow."

Jim was on his knees giving it a close-up inspection and announced his diagnosis: "It's not stain—it's shellac."

"Can we get it off?" I asked.

"No," Jim said. "Shellac doesn't come off. You're stuck with it." My eyes welled with tears. "Boy," Jim continued as he touched it, "he didn't even sand the rungs before he shellacked either. It's sticky, and look at all those drips."

"I think I'm going to cry," I said.

"Come outside and look at the cement pad," Immy coaxed, trying to take our mind off the banister disaster. "It'll make you feel better. We finished it only yesterday."

But it only made me feel worse.

"Look at all that mud!" I moaned. "We can't walk through mud every time we want to get to the hot tub."

"Yes, we can," Scott said, speaking from his wallet. "We'll put a couple of boards down and wait until the grass grows in."

"Grass?" I frowned. "This shouldn't be grass. This should be a patio. Am I right, Immy?"

"A patio would be very nice with a large square of old English boxwood for privacy and a few stands of white rubrum lilies just over there…" Scott went back inside to stare at the banister.

That night, after inspecting our banister from every angle, I sat down in the shower and just cried. Actually, I wailed. "It's not that bad," Scott said, knocking on the door. "Come out Bruce. Come out right now. It's not that bad!"

"That makes me feel worse." I sobbed. "It proves you have NO TASTE!" A little while later, Scott knocked again. "Leave me alone!" I yowled. "Just leave me alone!"

"But there's a phone call for you."

"I don't want to talk to…" And then the phone, followed by Scott's arm, invaded the bathroom. Angrily, I dried my hand on a towel and grabbed the phone. "Hello?" I chirped happily, giving my best southern-turn-on-a-dime performance.

"Bruce, this is Lisa Miller," the caller said.

"Yes?" Hours of inhaling the smell of shellac had removed any recognition of the *Blue Stone Press* editor's name.

"I just wanted to let you know about a *little* issue that's come up…" She went on to explain that I had become the local headline. My fourth column in the paper—the one about our friend's real estate shopping experience and the real estate agent who desperately tried to make the sale—had caused a small town scandal. Everyone was pointing fingers at local realtors and debating a very important question: just who was this mysterious shyster I dubbed "Jabba the Hutt?" And, perhaps more frighteningly for me, what does Bruce Littlefield look like?

"Don't worry, I'm standing by you," Lisa promised after telling me that the column had doubled the paper's circulation. She was happy to report that every single copy had sold out. "But you should know that in next week's paper there are a couple letters to the editor about you, including one from your friends who almost bought that house you wrote about." She paused as my heart dropped. "And I should probably also tell you that someone called and asked if you drive a red Fiero."

The weekend the "Jabba column," as it came to be known, was published, our "best" friends happened to be looking at some other houses. Their new real estate agent pointedly asked them if they were the people who had looked at "the bog" with "Jabba the Hutt." After finding out that they indeed were, she had promptly dumped them as clients.

Our friends' letter to the editor attempted to put distance between Mr. Littlefield, "the writer," and them, "the innocent home buyers." They lambasted me for finding humor in their near-tragic buy, even though we had all enjoyed a good laugh about it. I was hurt. To make worse matters worse, since I had not used their names in the column, they didn't want to sign their letter to the editor, hoping to avoid being ostracized by their neighbors when they finally did buy a house. "But," as Lisa explained, "according to the newspaper's policy, all letters to the editor must be signed. I told them that their only other option was to take out an ad."

They did. And I agreed to pay for it.

That night, while brushing my teeth, I griped to Scott, "I can't believe that I'm paying to be criticized."

"Look," Scott said, "you could reconsider your career. Maybe not be a writer anymore. Can't you find something to do with your life that *doesn't hurt anyone?*"

"What?" I snapped. "Like selling real estate?" I went to bed angry, but woke up with a new idea for my next column.

MOVING IN

By Bruce Littlefield

This week's column now comes to a screeching halt so that I may calm some troubled waters:

I have great respect for the real estate profession. In fact, not only is Scott a real estate broker, but a couple columns ago I made the real estate market buzz with how Raiza, our real estate goddess, had walked us into the perfect house on her first try! The yarn I wove last week was a sad real estate tale—one that seemed altogether contrary to what I think the real estate profession represents. In case you missed it, a house my friends were in the process of buying became waterlogged, and I felt the agent involved had deliberately tried to dodge the important questions floating around the house.

I described the real life comedy of a hungry agent working to make the deal while ignoring a whole bee's nest of problems. Not wanting to cause her career harm, but instead communicate the dramatic events that transpired, I maintained her anonymity by describing her as a character from science fiction named Jabba the Hutt.

As I've now been told, the column caused brouhahas at several local establishments the night it hit newsstands. I am also aware that papers got thrown around at the *Hasbrouck House*. Not to imply that the delightfully delicious *Hasbrouck House* has flies, but one barfly told me that, as fate would have it, much of the county's real estate sales force happened to be present and were all pouring over my column like Scotch over rocks. It seems in trying to figure out just who this Jabba woman was, and there was a lot of finger pointing. As I heard it, accusations were being passed around as freely as cocktail weenies at a family reunion.

What was left in the aftermath of the evening was a pile of strewn papers, some misdirected allegations, and a few nasty hangovers. The first has been cleaned up, the latter slept off, but the middle is my dilemma.

By retelling the drama of good people led straight into marshy waters, I caused a tidal wave of hurt feelings and controversy. Certainly not my intention. I struggled for the answer to the hot spot I found myself in. I needed to find a voice of guidance, and I realized she was sitting on the last page of the *Bluestone Press* wearing pearls and smiling at me.

HOROSCOPES by Judy Goldstein

I dialed the number for one of Judy's advertised "private readings." A soothing voice answered, and I introduced myself. "Yes, I know who you are," she said. *Uh oh, she's heard*, I thought. "And I love your column!"

I recounted the charges against me: First, I had told a tale out of school. Next, to protect my story's villain, I changed her name to a meanie from *Star Wars* known to eat alien frogs. So, everyone in the county started trying to figure out who Jabba the

Hutt is, and are altogether missing my "Let the buyer beware" point of it all. And now, I'm feeling like Luke Skywalker about to be thrown into the pit. Then, I decided to go ahead and give Judy Goldstein the worst of it. "Okay, Judy, there's one more thing…" I said. "I used the word 'slovenly.' And apparently you should never refer to a woman as slovenly, even if she is."

Judy jumped into action. "What sign are you?" she asked eagerly.

"Libra. I need balance."

"I *seeeee*," she said slowly.

I argued my case: "Doesn't it help that slovenly really means 'careless.' It's right there in the *Oxford Dictionary*."

"I don't know anything about that."

"Oh," I said, making a note so I could work that into my column. "I really meant to describe her callus performance, not necessarily her physicality." I waited through a long moment of silence. Nothing. "So, Judy," I urged, hoping for her engine to jumpstart, "what advice can you give me?"

"First, I need some information." *Uh-oh*, I hoped she wasn't going to ask me if I drive the red Fiero or for my street address.

"Where were you born?" she asked.

"South Carolina."

"What town? What time? What day? What year?" And then her questions stopped.

"I'll work this up," she said and promised to call me back in a few hours after she took "a good look at the stars." I peered out the kitchen window and there wasn't a star in sight.

I nervously paced around the house like an expectant father, waiting for Judy's call. My mind jumped from one question to another. Will my tires get slashed? Will Storm Troopers overtake my yard and annihilate my new Japanese maple? Will my dear gardener Immy refuse to take out the remaining poison ivy still threatening to take down my large maple tree. Am I going to be nachoed and feathered the next time I eat at the Egg's Nest Saloon? Can I still buy simple screws on sale in the Marbletown True Value?!

When the phone rang, I jumped. Judy began the conversation dramatically. "Well," she said, "you should know that Mercury is sitting on the south node."

"Get it off!" I chuckled.

"This is a serious answer," she said, quickly putting an end to my laugh. "You are a talented young man, and since you were born in the early evening…"

"Um," I interrupted, "I was born at five o'clock in the morning."

"Oh," she said, obviously surprised. "I thought you said 'five in the evening.' Well, no trouble, I'll just read it upside down." I heard the shuffling of papers in her hand. "You were a writer in a past life, you know," she continued. "No doubt you were very famous."

I quickly jotted down the "famous" part for another conversation. "But," I asked, "will people be able to see I didn't mean any personal harm when I wrote that column—that I was only trying to bring out the humor in a swampy situation?"

"A gentle reminder," her kind voice replied. "You can't step on toes in a small town, even accidentally."

"What do you think will happen to me?" I held my breath.

"You have Venus and Jupiter on the ascendant," she said. "So only good things are going to happen to you." I let out an audible "phew!" that made Jasper raise his head to listen. "You're on the road to being a famous writer again."

"But what about Jabba and all that?"

"This Jabba mess will soon pass. We'll all move on," she said. "You need to allow good things to happen by going forth. As your horoscope says this week, 'You are a natural leader and storyteller. Use this quiet time to tap into your well of creativity in a practical way and forget past disappointments.'"

"The real question," I asked quietly, "is should I carry on with my column?"

"Of course! You have Gemini in the tenth house!" she enthused. "You like busying yourself and are meant to be a busy person with too much on your plate. When met with disappointment, you can shelve it all and go onto different grounds. But over the next few days, you'll not rest easily. It'll only last a few days."

I hung up with Judy and immediately called our disappointing contractor and fired him. I was going to move onto other grounds. Then, I called Immy and Jim to tell them we did need a patio, and followed that by writing my sixty-dollar check for an ad in the *Blue Stone Press* so Bonnie and Rob could anonymously annihilate me. That night, I slept rough. Judy Goldstein's predictions were dancing around in my head. But the following day, I cranked out my new column and sent it to press.

Once renovated and decorated with garage sale finds, the cottage overlooking the creek became my one of my favorite spots to write my column.

7

HOW TO SKIN A CAT

I got over the hurt of criticism with two good painkillers—wine and shopping. After a few sips and not enough spits at a wine tasting in Stone Ridge, I told Scott to follow the red arrows on the "antiques" sign to Cat House Antiques.

I was giddy as I walked in and saw the treasure trove of vintage 20th Century Beauties on display—an instant *mee-yow*! I turned to the cheerful woman with merlot-red hair standing behind the counter. "Is the Madame here?" I inquired.

"You've found her," she said. "Want to take home one of my girls?" Her furniture and wares were exactly my taste and our senses of humor came together like two dogs in heat.

"Well, which is the hottest?" I teased.

"You're welcome to look around and fondle them."

An anxious looking Scott interrupted our banter. "Can I use your bathroom?" he asked with a panicked expression.

"I'm sorry. I don't have one," Madame replied.

Scott gave me the eye, and we walked over and stood in the corner next to a collection of salt and peppershakers and an assortment of green glassware that, by the price, I was sure had a name.

We conferenced:

"I have *got* to go to the bathroom," he pleaded. "And I can't believe she doesn't have a bathroom here. Where does she go?"

"We're in a converted two-car garage," I whispered, not taking my eyes off an atomic glassware set. "Just how bad do you have to go?"

"Really bad," he said squirming. "All that wine we had is running to the finish line."

I showed my usual lack of sympathy. "Can't you just cross your legs for a little while?" I asked. "If I leave the store now, someone might come in and buy the things I want!"

"What is it you want?" he asked, crossing his legs.

"That!" I said, walking over to read the tag. "It's a 1930's Napanee Electrified Kitchenette, in perfect condition." The inside panels were inscribed with measurement conversions, household hints, and things worth knowing. I instantly knew she was the one for me.

"And it's got a light," Scott said, his bladder making some room for interest. Who knew a light could calm an aching bladder. "How much is..." Suddenly, his head spun faster than an original Oster blender. "Look at that table," he said bending towards a 1930s black and white enamel top table with four matching white chairs.

"Conference," I said as again we moved back toward the collection of salt and peppershakers and the plates somebody collects. "Stop looking! Don't make it so obvious, or she'll never budge on the price."

"Should we get the pie safe *and* the table?" he asked, knowing my answer.

"You or me? Who's going to do the negotiation?"

"You," he said. "You are much better at it than me."

I calmly walked toward Madame's perch and, looking not the least bit interested, I casually glanced at a lamp, lifted the lid of a pink canister, and rang an old cowbell.... Then, I threw out, "What kind of deal could you give us on the pie safe and the table set?"

"Hmmmm," she purred. "Those are my best pieces. You obviously have a good eye."

Did I sound too desperate and could she see through my veneer? She pulled out her calculator, punched in some numbers, wrote a figure on a torn piece of brown paper, and slid it across the counter.

I lifted the slip off the counter as if it was the final slip in a who-gets-the-last-seat-in-the-lifeboat draw.

I picked it up, examining it closely. Realizing it was upside down, I flipped it over and crisply announced, "Sold."

"I'm Beverly," the Madame of Cat House Antiques said as we shook hands on the deal.

"I'm Bruce Littlefield."

"You're a wanted man in these parts! But don't worry. I won't turn you in! I found your column funny."

"Oh! Does that get me a bigger discount?"

"No, but your friend there can use the bathroom inside the house."

"Hey Scott! My column gets us bathroom privileges."

"Except at a few places," Beverly laughed and then quickly turned to escort a squirming Scott to her house.

Scott returned just in time to watch me sign the check.

Beverly told us to look carefully at the placards posted inside our newly purchased cabinet: "'Household hints,'" I read. "'To remove fruit stains, pour boiling water over stained surface having it fall from a distance of three feet.' Three feet, sounds tricky! 'For a burn, apply equal parts of white of egg and olive oil mixed together and then cover with a piece of old linen.'" Then, the addendum to the cure-a-burn directions: "'If applied at once, no blister will form.'

"Really charming," I said, and then I pictured our first fight: *Quick, Scott! I've burned my hand! Get me an egg—no, not the yolk—only the whites!* Not *Pam. Olive oil! Where's the olive oil? That dishrag isn't linen, and the directions clearly say linen!* It would end with me screaming through the pain—*Why are all our dishcloths polyester?!*

Scott turned the handle of the flour sifter. "We have a beautiful peach tree in our yard that's loaded with peaches!" he said. "I can't wait to make peach pies on that thing."

"Oh no!" I said. "I'm remembering your 'forgotten cookies' from last Christmas. Those things were so heavy I individually wrapped them and gave them out as paperweights."

"I'm planning to learn to bake!" Scott said with a huff. "It'll be fun."

I turned my attention back to our new cabinet. "And here are 'Things worth knowing,'" I read. "'Three and one half pounds of uncooked chicken will make one heaping quart of diced meat after boiling! One and one half pounds of butter will spread 100 slices of bread for sandwiches.' Who needs to butter a hundred slices of bread?!

"'In preparing for a church supper for 200'—ha! Aren't we all?—'it will be necessary to provide ten loaves of white bread, eight loaves of brown and eight pounds of butter. Also, nine three quart pans of scalloped oysters, two twelve pound hams, six gallons of chicken salad, six pounds of coffee, five pounds of sugar, two gallons of cream, seven gallons of ice-cream and nine cakes.'"

While I continued to read the side of our new furniture, Scott was searching through dishware and found a set of vintage Pyrex bowls that he felt would be just right for mixing his dough for his newfound baking hobby. We were ready to go home with our treasures. And it was only then that I looked outside and saw our little red two-seater that everyone in town was on the lookout for. "Uh-oh," I said. "Pardon me, Madame, but do you deliver?"

8

GETTING A WOODY

After trying to squeeze one newfound treasure too many into our one-box-is-one-box-too-many car, we decided to look for another car—one that suited "the country." Nothing fancy, we just needed space. But if it could be a four-wheel drive Jeep Grand Wagoneer with wood paneled sides and lots of space, I knew I'd be happy!

Last Sunday morning, after Immy and Jim finished the third tilling of our soon-to-be garden, we asked them to keep their eyes peeled for a real Woody. I knew they got around the countryside a lot and thought they might spot one.

On Monday, our phone rang back in the city. "Well, we found your car," Immy said gleefully.

I bit my lower lip. "Is it for sale?" I asked.

"Yes!!!" Then the story: "Jim and I were getting gas at the Mobil station, and Jim saw it passing. He started waving his arms in the air to get the driver's attention, and can you believe it? She turned around and pulled right over! I would have never pulled over myself, as you never know what kind of freak could be trying to get you to pull over. And for who knows what?! Anyway, it had Florida plates and the woman gave Jim her phone number."

I pinched myself. Mild pain. I wasn't dreaming. I thanked Immy, hung up, and immediately dialed the lady from Florida. My heart revved. "Hi there! My name is Bruce Littlefield, and my friends saw your Grand Wagoneer up in Ulster County today. I've always wanted one, and they told me you're planning to sell yours. Could you tell me a little about the car?"

"Hold on," the voice said. "Let me get my Mom." The phone dropped to the sound of "*Maaaahuum!* … There's a man on the phone about the car."

I repeated myself to the notably more adult voice, leaving out the please-charge-me-a-lot tone and the "I've-always-wanted-one" price hiker.

"What do you want to know?" the woman asked, seeming to giggle a bit.

I was stumped. "What color is it?" I asked, instantly giving away my expired subscription to *Car Digest*. She said the car was black, and so I asked the only other question I could think of—"So, how much are you asking?"

She named her price, quickly adding, "But I know how much I'll take for it."

I realized she was as inexperienced at used car negotiation as I am. So, my big city voice kicked back in. "What's wrong with it?" I demanded.

Then she told me the history, or her version, of the black Jeep Grand Wagoneer with wood paneled sides that she bought in Florida. "We got it last year to drive up north with our two dogs, cats, and our bird…" I faded out as she described the wood-paneled Noah's Ark that made its way north and daydreamed of driving to the Home Depot to pick up mulch. My mind was on I-want-it cruise control.

I hung up and called Scott over and quickly described the car. "What year is it?" he asked.

"Ummm. Vintage?"

"Well, what kind of engine does it have?" he asked like he knew engines.

"I don't know the number, but she said her husband said it had a big engine! She couldn't remember which V it was. But she said it was definitely powerful." Scott asked then more rapid-fire questions, each answered with another "I don't know!"

Finally, I remembered an important detail that Scott hadn't even asked about. "It has power windows!" I thought that would do the trick, but instead, it was decided I needed to call her back.

"Hi, it's me, Bruce, again. Can I ask you a few more questions?"

"Sure!" she said, giggling like my best friend.

I ticked through Scott's list: Year? How many miles? Power brakes? Power steering? Radio? Air conditioning? Luggage rack? Gas mileage? Interior? And the tank-draining stumper: "Why are you selling it?"

"I'm not going to lie to you," she said. "My husband found a van for fifty dollars."

"Excuse me? Did you say, 'fifty dollars?'" She giggled some more.

"I'll call you back," I said. I had already decided that the car, like the house we walked into and bought as real estate virgins, was meant to be. I want it. I want it. I want it. I gave Scott his answers: "1988. 136,000 miles. Yes! Yes, with CD, of course. Yes! Beige, and it's leather. And she says they don't need it because they found a van for fifty bucks."

"I want to have it inspected," Scott said with final authority.

"I can't ask her to let us have it inspected!" I rattled back.

"I've discussed it with my mother and she says we have to have it looked at." His mother—the woman whose very definition of recycling is getting herself a new car every year—wants us to have it inspected? Maybe I should have her ask Ms. Grand Wagoneer that? Do people really have used cars inspected?

"Hi, me again, Bruce," I started rather timidly. "We're really interested in the car, but would it be at all possible to have someone look at it?"

She easily agreed and said she would come over for coffee later that week, and we could take it to any mechanic we liked. We could firm up the details later. "We may move between now and then," she added. "But I'll take your number and call you if our number changes."

Two days later I got nervous and called. No answer. *Somebody else had seen the car, offered more, and drove it away—without an inspection. No,* I reassured myself, *she's just not answering her call waiting*. Five minutes later, I called again. No answer. *Maybe I insulted her when I said we wanted someone to look at it*. I tried again and still no answer. *Did she just plain get up and move and forget about me?* I hit redial—no answer. I repeated this scenario many times over the next twenty-four hours. No answer. So, I finally came to terms with the fact that she had flown the coop and my dream car had driven away.

The next day the phone rang and it was Ms. Wagoneer. She said my number had come up a couple of times on her caller ID. She apologized for taking so long to get back to me. "I thought you had already sold it," I announced pathetically.

"Oh, no," she said. "If anyone was interested, and no one was, I was going to tell them you had to see it first."

When she drove the car over, Scott was picking peaches and again threatening to make peach pies. Ms. Wagoneer bragged that she had a great peach pie recipe to share with Scott, and we made small talk. She used to breed German shepherds and horses, but decided grey mice were her real passion. She also loved antiques. During a recent past life regression with a psychic in Florida, she had even described some pyramid in Egypt room by room! Finally, we talked about the car. "There's a little oil leak," she confessed causing an audible gurgle in my stomach. "It's nothing serious, and my husband said he would easily fix it for you."

"I think that's very nice of him," I reassured Scott as we drove our potential car to our car doctor. While they checked Woody's vital organs for signs of disease or denting or something, I paced outside in the waiting room. The mechanic finally announced his prognosis: "You have a leak in the rear seal and another one in the front. The parts are only about three dollars each, but it's a major job because we have to take out the transmission to get at them. There are also signs of leakage in the fuel pump, but it doesn't seem to be leaking now."

Hmmmm, I thought. *Is that bad?*

He went on to say that Wagoneers are great cars with high resale values, and in his opinion, he'd try to get it for a lower price and then make the repairs. After we promised to never use the trick back on him, he told us exactly what to do: "Say you're interested, but given it has some problems, you think the price is a little high. And then ask her what she'd take. Once she names her price, do some quick math and jump a few hundred dollars lower. You'll settle on something in between. Got it?"

When we sat down with Ms. Wagoneer, I launched into my script. "The little oil leak turns out to be actually quite big," I said, wheeling and dealing like a pro. "We're still interested, but what would you take for it?"

"Um," she countered, "what do you think is fair?"

Oh no! The car doctor didn't tell me how to handle this twist. I looked over to Scott. He shrugged his shoulders and looked back at me. I looked at her and blurted out "one thousand nine hundred and fifty-five dollars?"

"Okay," she said. And, as quick as that, our negotiation was over. We had just bought a twelve-year-old car with a major oil leak, and what did I do? I hugged her!

9

GAS & ELECTRIC

When our speckled blue Jacuzzi was delivered, Immy and Jim met the electrician at the house so he could run the line from the basement to the new cement pad. They would lay the patio later. I had secretly whispered to Immy making sure that Scott was out of earshot that I wanted the electrician to run a line out into the garden. "I'm sure we'll eventually want to install some lights once the garden is in."

I drove up to the country midweek to go out plant shopping with Immy. I also wanted to get the Jacuzzi filled and ready for Scott, so I could gloat, "I told you we can't live without this Jacuzzi." Ms. Wagoneer had left a basket on our front porch full of all the ingredients needed for making a peach pie. She had also included a handmade and illustrated recipe book with this inscription: "May your home be filled with sweet kindness and love." Inside were all the how-to's for peach pie, peach cobbler, peach preserves, peach Melba, peach kuchen, peach ice-cream… enough to keep us peachy for the rest of the year, maybe even for our lives.

I dropped the basket on the table and ran outside. There she was! A cedar-encased cauldon of happiness, and a calendar full of steamy nights waiting to be had! Just as he'd promised, the electrician had obviously been there. It was hooked up and plugged in. I carefully lifted the cover. No water yet. So, I wrestled the hosepipe out of the basement and began filling the tub. As the water splashed into the Jacuzzi's faux granite shell, I couldn't help but think—*I'm going to be a homemaking hero.*

As the Jacuzzi filled, I went inside to start dinner, or at least try. I'm not a trained cook and my specialty is frozen French fries. It was my sister who made them legendary in her third grade essay titled, "I love my brother because he makes the best frozen French fries in the whole world."

I pulled the bag out of our sorry-excuse-for-a-refrigerator that came with our house. I hadn't really noticed the refrigerator when we looked at the house because I was too busy adoring the magnificence of the antique cast iron stove. The stove was capable of cooking by coal, by wood or by gas. It was very unique, extremely charming, and Scott wanted it gone as soon as we closed on the house. I had insisted on keeping it, and the burners boiled water quite well. We had not yet attempted to light the oven.

I opened the heavy door to peek inside. As there were no buttons or pilot lights, I called Immy, but she wasn't home. So, I called Bev at Cat House Antiques, because I knew she knew antiques.

"Cat House," she purred.

"Hey, Bevy! It's Bruce Littlefield, and I'm getting ready to roll out pie dough on our pie safe..."

"What pie safe?" she asked.

"Our pie safe," I reminded her. "The one we bought from you."

"That's not a pie safe," she said, explaining that pie safes are a lot more simplistic than what I have. "They're basically just cabinets with a screen door on them so that the pies can cool safely away from flies. But yours..." Madame said proudly of her former enamel-topped girl sitting in my kitchen, "is a Hoosier—an electrified Hoosier. And it isn't even really a Hoosier. The Hoosier brand did all the advertising, so the cabinets became known as Hoosier, like tissues became Kleenex. Yours is a top of the line 1930's Napanee Electrified Kitchenette."

"Well, I'm really not making pies anyway," I admitted. "I'm making French fries, and I need to know how to turn on my oven."

"Sounds challenging," she said. "There should be a little hole inside, on the bottom. Turn on the gas and light the hole."

"Is that where the broilers are?"

"The what?"

"The broilers," I repeated. "Do I stick the flame right against the broilers?"

"Broilers are chickens that don't lay eggs," she cackled.

I glanced outside. "Oh no! My hot tub is overflowing. Gotta go!" I ran outside and sloshed through the mud puddle that had now overtaken our backyard. "Damnit!" I cried out loud to the heavens. "Now, how am I going to get Scott into the hot tub?"

By the time I stopped the water and figured out the precise recipe for ph balance this and clarifier that, I was really hungry. I took off my muddy shoes, tiptoed to the stove, and turned on the gas. I heard the *sshhhh* of gas as it entered the chamber, so I struck a match and held it over the little hole. Nothing happened. I turned the gas higher and heard a bigger *SSShhhhh*. I struck another match and again held it over the little hole. Nothing still.

I closed the oven door thinking perhaps the gas needed to build up for a second. I opened the door, peered deep into the back of the oven, and noticed a little hole way back there. *Maybe that's it*, I thought, leaning in and striking a match. *BOOOOF!* A boom of an explosion, lots of blue light, and then the distinctive odor of burnt hair. I ran into the bathroom and looked in the mirror. Fortunately, all my hair was still intact. "Wow," I told Jasper twenty-five minutes later as I proudly ate my fries. "I did it!"

The next morning, I climbed into Immy's big truck to go plant shopping and discovered that my French fries had not come without cost. "What happened to your eyebrow?" Immy asked, leaning toward me and squinting to get a better look.

"What eyebrow?" I asked as I flipped her rearview mirror toward me.

"The eyebrow over your left eye. *It's missing*." Yep, I had singed off half an eyebrow. But the truth is, it was worth it. I still felt the great satisfaction of my very first home-cooked meal.

That afternoon when Immy dropped me off, I immediately went around back to the hot tub and eagerly threw back the cover. I expected to feel a steamy waft of awaiting relaxation, but what I found instead were troubled waters. I ran inside and pulled out the tub's instruction manual. Across the front in red bold-faced letters was: "DO NOT PLUG IN UNLESS FILLED WITH WATER."

"Oh, no!" I cried. "Please tell me no."

"Yes indeed," Immy confirmed an hour later. "He must have plugged it in."

"Who is this crackpot, anyway?!" I asked, my temper hotter than the temperature my Jacuzzi should be. "Call him right now and tell him he's in hot water! And I mean hot water! I'm reporting him to the… to the… I'm reporting him to somebody that's going to… Immy! Oh God! Scott is going to kill me!"

As Immy called the electrian, I called Home Depot. "My hot tub was delivered yesterday, and it isn't working."

"Is it plugged in, sir?" the man asked.

"Oh, yes, it's plugged in," I answered honestly. "Has been since yesterday."

"Is there any power?"

"Yes, the little orange light is on."

"Will the bubbles bubble?" he asked.

"Yes, but the water is not heating."

"Hmmmm," he said. "Sounds like the heating element is defective."

"Yes, I'm sure it's something like that," I eagerly agreed.

"We'll bring you out another one before noon tomorrow and make an even exchange."

I called Immy to share the good news. "And you tell Bozo the Electrician I never want to see his face *again*!" Then, remembering I'd never actually met him, I added, "Ever. At all. I never want to even know what he looks like. And he better go to Lowe's from now on because I've told Home Depot to be on the lookout for him." The electrician joined the contractor on my black list of people who would never get invited to a party.

When Scott arrived at the country on Friday night, we walked across the planks Immy and Jim had carefully placed over the mud and slipped into the steamy water. "Isn't this absolutely the best?" I asked as the bubbles danced about. "And what a beautiful night!"

"Amazing," Scott sighed, settling into the water and looking skyward as a gentle breeze blew. After a few moments of silence, he asked, "What's that?"

"What's what?"

"Is that a dead tree hanging right over our heads?" Our thirty seconds of bubbly bliss was over. "I think we should get out before it falls on us."

10

SOFA DEAL

After Scott wrote the one thousand three hundred dollar check for the tree removal, I happily pointed out, "Well, we would have probably spent that on firewood anyway! And don't you feel so much better knowing that it's not going to slam down on our heads?"

"True," he agreed. Now that the tree was down we could really relax in our Jacuzzi. We found it was pretty much the only place we could relax. We certainly weren't relaxing on our sofa ensemble. Since we had unloaded them from the U-Haul, I don't think I'd sat back down on them again. Our ensemble was involved in a saga all their own.

The or*deal* began before we even owned the house, at Bloomingdale's One Day Sale. Carolyn, our salesperson, was a Pressure Professional. You've experienced the type: *Buy it now! Or pay thousands more tomorrow.*

"I love the color—it's *caramel*," she cooed as Scott and I stared at the overstuffed ensemble of four. "It will match any décor and with the quartet, you really have a whole room."

"Maybe we don't need *four* pieces," Scott said practically. "After all, we haven't even closed on our house, much less measured the living room."

"Well, *separately*," she said, caressing the furniture like Janice on *The Price is Right*, "these pieces would sell for close to four thousand dollars, but *today* at our One Day Sale, the entire set can be yours for less than seventeen hundred dollars." (A *dollar* less, but I'll give her that.)

"Does it only come in caramel?" I asked.

"No, it also comes in *forest*," she revealed. "But I'll have to check on how long that will take." She stared at me over the rim of her black reading glasses, trying to hypnotize me with her *You-want-it-in-caramel* eyes.

"Find out how long forest will take," I glared back with my baby blues. "We're not moving in for a while."

She yanked her glasses from her face and left to check on forest. Scott and I had a few moments to bounce around on the furniture and sit with the idea that these could be in a living room of a house we didn't actually own yet. "Will all this fit in there?" I asked as I reclined on the sofa.

"I guess so," Scott said from the chair. "Do you like the tan?"

"*Caramel*," I said, puffing my lips and mimicking Carolyn's breathiness. Scott chuckled, then choked. I looked up from my repose to see Carolyn and her stack of blonde hair peeping down at me. Her fuel-injected lips weren't laughing.

"Forest will take five weeks."

I wallowed into upright. "We need to talk about it for a minute," I said. She didn't move. "Alone."

Since she obviously was staying by the showpieces, Scott and I journeyed over to the bureaus and armoires section. I gasped at the price tag of an armoire I liked. "*Seven thousand dollars?* Who in their right mind would pay seven thousand dollars for that?" I noticed a salesclerk shooting me eye darts. He was showing a young couple the matching piece.

"Ooops," I apologized. "My bad." Scott and I ducked over to beds. "Are we alone?"

"What do you have in mind?" he toyed.

"Be serious. Do you like it in caramel or should we wait for forest?"

"Well, forest won't get so dirty," he said. Always practical.

"Yes, but with all our windows, forest might fade."

"Good point," he agreed. We quickly headed for Carolyn and her Four Piece Quartet—One Day was almost over. We told her of our concerns with the Fading Forest and gave her the nod to place an order for the Caramel Delight.

"I think you should consider the Guardsman Warranty," she continued selling. "If you spill anything on it, get it dirty, split it, scratch it, gash it, whatever—they'll come out and fix it for free. And if they can't clean it or repair it, they will replace it."

Scott got to the real point: "How much?"

"$232.74."

Scott and I agreed that with Jasper's paws and our friends, it might be a good investment. Carolyn gave us our total, and then added, "Delivery is just fifty dollars extra."

"You'd think when you're spending this much, they'd deliver it for free," I cheaped.

"You're getting such a deal," Carolyn whispered, as if she was letting us steal it. "What's your zip code?"

"Billing or delivery," I said, for the first time realizing we were now a *two* zip code family.

"Delivery."

Scott and I riffled through our papers. We didn't know if the house was in Stone Ridge, Marbletown, or Kingston. We had seen all of them listed on various documents, so we guessed: "12404?"

"*Oh*," Carolyn moaned. "That's not in the city? Delivery is going to be a little more." She got out her calculator and picked up the phone. "Yes." She entered some numbers. "No." She talked on the phone. "Yes." She looked up. "Okay." She hung up and said, "Delivery is seven hundred forty two dollars and fifty cents."

"Deal breaker!" I announced dramatically. "Scott, let's go." Carolyn followed us through rugs toward the elevator, offering options and reminding us that the One Day Sale ended tomorrow. Then, I had a brainstorm. We were getting a U-Haul anyway. *Why not have their movers load it right into our U-Haul?*

And that's what we'd done. The day we moved, we loaded up the shrink-wrapped sofa set with our new pots, pans, and a vacuum, and we drove the U-Haul on a No Trucks Allowed highway to our new house.

As we unwrapped the last bit of tape on the sofa set, we had a crisis:

"Look!" I screeched. "Lipstick!" A distinctive pink lipstick stain graced the back of the sofa, and I knew Scott and I weren't wearing any.

"And look at this!" Scott yelled. "A rip!"

We stared at each other in the day's unifying moment, and together we shrieked: "*Floor model*!"

After that, One Day Sale Carolyn's name was mud. Not only would Bloomingdale's not clean our sofas, but they also wouldn't even acknowledge the sofas existed. Bottom line: After two days of torturous dealings with digitally answered, press number-one-for-this, two-for-that customer service lines, we were stuck with the ensemble.

Days came and went and Bloomingdale's did nothing. I threatened to file a report with the Better Business Bureau, but days turned into weeks. Bloomingdale's said that they'd send someone out to clean the sofas. A man did come. He looked at our sofas, said he'd "order parts," and we never heard from him again. I threatened that "I'll see Carolyn in Small Claims Court," but still no solution.

Summer solstice passed. Finally, Bloomingdale's began to weaken. A man called and announced, "Mr. Littlefield, we've decided to bring you all new sofas." But, he added, "The delivery charge will be seven hundred forty two dollars and fifty cents because they aren't at the original address of delivery."

"The original address was a U-Haul," I explained. "And they're sitting in the house we bought them for!"

Bloomingdale's Customer Service Supervisor Gloria, extension 2736, was now assigned our case. "Tell me the story from the beginning," the raspy-voiced, furniture Judge Judy said. I told my saga yet again and ended with a dramatic "and if my sofas aren't here by Christmas, I'm writing a scathing article in a home magazine that my friend edits!"

Judge Gloria's verdict was rendered immediately: "Even exchange! And they'll be there within the month."

Arranging delivery was another annoying challenge. Two scheduled deliveries were cancelled: the first for weather problems, the second because "the truck was too full." When the two stooges finally arrived to deliver the set, it became obvious they needed, and were missing, *the third.* After backing their truck into a tree in our driveway, Larry and Moe marched in with the new sofa and stacked it precariously on top of the old sofa so they could get out the old ottoman. When Moe asked me to open the door, I said, "I think I should hold that sofa. It looks to me like it's going to fall."

"No, you get the door," Moe barked at me. "And we get the furniture."

So, I got the door as instructed, and they walked toward me pulling the ottoman. Just as I predicted, the Tower of Sofas crashed into the wall, sliding down the framed wall mirror and taking out the lamp my mother had given me for my birthday.

Aaaaahhhhh! I shrieked at the rubble beneath the sofa.

"Give me that lamp," Moe said, as Larry ducked for cover. "I fix it!"

"Oh no! No! I'm running the show now," I said. "Just lift the sofa!" They lifted the sofa. I pulled the lamp carcass from beneath the sofa. Its long neck was snapped, and its sleek ceramic body broken in too many places. I waved the pancaked shade at Moe. "I don't think you'll fix it."

After a heated telephone call with management, the moving company agreed to replace my lamp. So, I began the quest to find the perfect replacement to match my caramel-colored sofa set. Then I heard the good news: Bloomingdale's was having a One Day Sale the very next week.

11

NOW AND ZEN

Rather than tackling the more serious structural problems in the house, Scott and I decided to slap a quick coat of paint on a few rooms and call it a weekend. A quick and easy thought turns into a drawn out and painful application. What is it about painting that always seems so simple, but immediately becomes all-consuming?

First, there are too many choices. All those dang paint colors: *Chocolate Foam*, *Chocolate Fizz*, *Milk Chocolate*.... Along with too many finishes: *Matte*, *Flat*, *Eggshell*, *Semi*.... And it's *messy*—there are buckets that get kicked and rollers guaranteed to spit their paint at you. They were and they did. It is downright *tedious*—unscrewing and not losing the tiny outlet screws and then feeling like a four-year-old trying to color within the lines. In the course of the first hour, I lost three screws as well as my mind.

Our plan for our Zen room (we had taken to giving the rooms in our house a name, perhaps as a way to encourage us to get it done faster) was to emulate an effect I'd seen on Tommy Tune's walls in the city. He had paid an interior designer megabucks to craft a wall that looked like the patina of the Parthenon. We figured that if it was tasteful enough for Athena, Goddess of Wisdom, and Tommy, God of Tap, it was tasteful enough for the Zen room at Edgewater Farm.

"We can do it ourselves," I had said confidently. "All we have to do is follow the instructions in our *Home Decorating Bible.*" (An impulse purchase that had, up to that point, never been used. And, after this episode, might not ever be used again.)

As instructed in *The Bible*, we had chosen a dark, rich "Ground Clove" as our base color—and I had coated the entire room in it. Three times. In semi-gloss. *Ohhhmmm.*

The plan was to *achieve Zen* by then rubbing the dark glossy walls with a creamy wash called "White Pigeon." We'd create Parthenon walls for our Zen room for the cost of two gallons of paint. Well, three. (After reading in the *Home Decorating Bible* that the wash coat needed to be mixed with a glaze, I bought a gallon of Faux Glaze mixture—an overpriced sauce that I told the salesperson was "probably just polyurethane and water.") *Ohhhhhhmmmmmmm.*

"Drag it straight down," Scott coached as I stroked the wall with the high-priced, slanty-bristled *technique* brush I'd bought. "Make it look like a waterfall."

"The paint isn't sticking to the wall," I complained. "It's glooping off the brush and sliding down my arm." The only thing getting glazed was my arm hair.

"Maybe you're using too much," Scott offered. He grabbed the brush and lightly feathered it in the can of paint. "The book said you should *dry brush*. I don't think you're dry brushing."

Scott whisked the brush down the wall in a determined, yet elegant, motion. His "dry brushing" created the look of a brown wall scrubbed with Ajax. We had each succeeded in royally messing up two sections of wall in a room I had prepared textbook perfect. I had given three asphyxiating evenings of my life to prepare the walls for "Technique" painting, and our two *techniques* had achieved a scratchy blur and the look of a frothy cesspool.

What happened next was more of a psychotic episode than any attempt at technique. Basically, we just went for it. We splashed paint on the wall. We ragged paint off the wall. We rubbed paint on with our hands. We rubbed paint off with steel wool. We even tried sticking sheets of Bounty paper towels—"the more absorbent quicker picker upper"—over freshly painted wall to soak up paint and provide texture. This technique, not in any book I assure you, left behind a geometric diamond pattern that was sort of appealing. We tried this technique for a while. After using 35 sheets of paper towel, we stood back and looked.

"Is that soothing?" Scott asked.

"Mesmerizing" was all my delirious head could conjure.

We realized we were insane. Well, Scott realized we were insane. I had gone to find the loofah sponge to see if that would render a better effect. By the time I returned, Scott was well on the way to what he thought was a masterpiece of Sistine Chapel proportions. He had continued with the dry brush recommendation—but a little less dry. The White Pigeon looked like streaks of pigeon poop. "What does that look like to you?" I asked Scott, attempting to measure his emotional and intellectual functioning.

"A white waterfall," he said.

"Scott, it looks like bad 1970's wallpaper."

"I like it," he insisted.

"It's a white EKG pattern on a dark backdrop!" I said, waving my White Pigeoned hands dramatically towards the wall. "How can *that* bring your mind to a state of meditation? Staring at that will put me over."

Ohmmmm. Ohhmmmm. Ohhhhmmmmm.

Our moment of silent meditation yielded another idea. "Let's just paint the whole thing a soothing color," I said, quickly running downstairs to get the pack of swatches I had squirreled away in a plastic folder like a junkie. I returned to the Zen room and dumped them on the floor. There were more colors than a box of Crayola 64. No, Crayola 128.

"Do we have to do this now?" Scott complained.

"We can pick a new color now," I decided strategically, "and go by Home Depot on our way to dinner."

We held swatch after swatch against the walls that were currently painted to arouse a coma. We agreed that "Midori" looked peaceful. Although, before we go any further in this story, I want it on record that I did raise an "it may be too pink" issue.

By the time we got to Home Depot, we were both twitchy. We had been inhaling paint for hours and had not eaten since breakfast. We stumbled over to the paint counter, and I gave the guy the Midori card number while Scott announced "flat" three times.

The mustached Homer looked at me. "Didn't you buy semi-gloss the other day?" he asked.

"Yes," I admitted.

"Are you painting over that?"

"Yes." Scott said. "*In flat.*"

"Well," Homer said, "you'll have to paint it first with primer or the gloss will come through." He turned and scooted off to mix the color. Scott glared at me.

"Look," I said, defending myself, "*The Bible* said, 'semi-gloss undercoat.' I didn't have a choice." When Homer opened the can to let us preview, all I could do was hum John Cougar Mellencamp's "Pink house, in the middle of the street. Pink house..."

"Shut-up," Scott laughed, as I moved away from the counter and headed toward the back of the store. "Hey, where are we going?"

"To put the salmon-in-a-can where it's supposed to be...on the discount shelf," I explained. "A Mary Kay saleslady will think she's found heaven when she buys a twenty dollar can of pink paint for three bucks."

"He mixed it for us, we should try it," Scott insisted. "I'm sure it'll be darker on the wall."

"Darker pink is mauve," I said. "I still think we should try Ralph Lauren's Suede." But seeing that Scott had moral reservations about leaving Midori for Mary Kay, I acquiesced. I grabbed a gallon of primer, and we headed for the checkout. "Last chance," I begged as the salmon slid down the counter toward the scanner. Quicker than you can say "*bleeep*," it was ours.

We rumbled back down our driveway as punchy as a giant bowl of pink lemonade. I jumped out of the Wagoneer, ran in the door, gave Jasper the three French fries I had saved him from my meal-at-the-mall crab cake sandwich, and ran upstairs. Armed with a new paintbrush and the can of salmon, I quickly stroked it on.

Once I'd gotten a big enough patch, I stepped back and took a look. "Scott!" I called. "Swim upstream, I mean, come upstairs and look!"

"No," he said. "I can tell by the way you're laughing it looks horrible."

"Not horrible. Just pink."

He walked in the room, and we both burst out laughing. After a few minutes of hooting, we agreed that a morning trip to Home Depot for Ralph Lauren "Suede" was in order. *Ohhhm-mmm.*

This tale ends with one thirty-two dollar gallon of Suede already soaked into the wall and at least one more gallon needed. But not this weekend, maybe next.

Hopefully, Scott and I will one day find peace in the Zen room. Could be that the greatest serenity would come by just shutting the door. (But, if you know a Mary Kay saleslady, I know where a gallon of pink paint is sitting on a discount shelf.)

12

WEST NILE

After a week of writing and real estating in the big city, we arrived in the country, as usual, on Friday night and, as usual, set about working. We were getting more rest in the city working than in the country resting, so I suggested we build a bonfire and insisted that we were going to sit by it, roast some marshmallows, and just relax for a little while.

With flashlight in hand, I went searching through the yard for kindling to start the fire. I bent down to pick up what I thought was a twig and stopped short. My fingers were inches from grabbing a large talon connected to a huge dead bird. I dropped the flashlight, let out a small *yelp*, and ran back to the house to get Scott.

Scott was already in the Zen room adding yet another coat of Suede to a wall. "Scott, Scott! Big bird... Dead." I said trying to catch my breath. "...Next to the woodpile."

"Who killed him?" Scott laughed as he calmly stroked the wall. "Elmo?"

"This is serious," I said. "There is a big dead bird next to the woodpile with talons the size of small branches."

"So, what does it look like?" Scott asked, not interested in anything besides finishing the *seventh*— and what we had decided was the *last*—coat of paint on the Zen room wall.

"Like this," I said, stiffening my hands arthritically and giving him the beady-eyed look of the dead bird. "Are you going to come see or not?"

Scott put down his brush with his this-better-be-good grunt. "Where's the flashlight?" he asked as we stepped out of the house into the pitch-blackness.

"I placed it next to the bird," I fibbed, making it sound as though I'd purposefully positioned the flashlight next to the dead bird as a beacon in the night.

We found the still lit flashlight near the still dead bird. "It's a hawk," Scott announced.

"How do you know?" I asked dumbly.

"The same way you know it's dead," he answered smugly. "It's obvious. Look at the features—the talons, the beak, the long tail feather."

"Oh. Well, don't get too close."

"Why not?" Scott asked spookily, shining the flashlight horrifically up his face. "What's it going to do—*come back from the dead and attack me?*"

"Stop it," I said. "I feel bad for the poor thing. How do you think it died?" I looked around suspiciously, not knowing if my newly hatched chill bumps were because I was cold or because Scott's horror movie face actually got to me.

"Maybe the hawk saw a mouse, and was coming in to grab it," he deduced, "but the hawk couldn't pull up from its dive soon enough. I'm thinking he slammed right into the woodpile and broke his neck."

His theory was very Sherlock Holmes, and I momentarily considered it. My theory was more panicky Nancy Drew, or maybe Daphne from Scooby Doo: "Scott, what if it had that mosquito thing that Immy is always talking about?"

"What mosquito thing?"

"The one from that river."

"What river?"

"You know. The river in Africa."

"Let's go to bed," Scott said giving up. "We'll bury it in the morning."

All night I worried about the hawk and how it died. Although Scott's theory sounded plausible, the one inside my head was more dramatic. And that's the one that was worrying me.

Shortly after dawn finally broke, I said, "*West Nile*!"

"What?" Scott asked, his eyes slowly opening.

"West Nile Virus! Birds in Westchester have it. How far is Westchester? I think we should call someone."

"I think we should just bury the bird," he said.

After breakfast Scott grabbed the shovel, and we headed behind the woodpile to prepare for our avian funeral. Scott was both gravedigger and pallbearer. We each said a prayer for the bird, Scott at graveside, me at a more plague-friendly distance. I secretly added an extra prayer about the mosquito thing. Once Scott covered our winged-friend with dirt, the interment was over and my thoughts of the West Nile Virus were buried. For the moment.

The following week, the same scenario occurred in our yard. Well, almost. It was a different dead animal. And it wasn't feathered—it was furred. And I didn't find it. Jasper did.

Jasper's dramatic howls called me outside, and I could see from a distance that Jasper had something backed up against the woodpile. "Jasper! Leave it!" I yelled as I ran across the yard. I had heard raccoons were mean, and often rabid. In this case, the raccoon was dead.

"You're not going to believe this," I told Scott as I dragged Jasper in the front door. "There is a dead raccoon in *exactly* the same spot the hawk was in." We rushed over to examine the scene, and this time even Scott kept his distance.

"The two have to be related," I insisted.

"Maybe there's a vortex," Scott said, applying for membership in my conspiracy club.

"Think about it," I sleuthed. "A mosquito could have bitten the hawk in Westchester and given it the West Nile Virus. Mosquitoes do bite birds."

"How do you know that?" Scott asked.

"Because this week I looked up some information on the Internet about mosquitoes and West Nile. Did you know that a mosquito beats its wings six hundred times per second, but only travels about one mile in an hour?"

"That's because it stops to give people the West Nile Virus along the way," Scott chuckled.

"You're not going to be laughing when you get West Nile," I said grimly.

"I'm sorry," Scott said, "but how again does a mosquito biting a hawk relate to a dead raccoon?"

"Don't you see? The mosquito could have bitten the hawk in Westchester, the hawk flew here, got sick and died by our woodpile..." and then I jumped to the logical conclusion, "...and the raccoon could have eaten the hawk."

"We buried the hawk," Scott said walking over to check on the gravesite. "It's undisturbed."

"Well, the raccoon could have nibbled on the hawk before we buried it," I insisted.

Scott agreed that we should ask someone what to do about the raccoon. So we decided to leave the raccoon, put Jasper in the house, and seek advice from someone in town. We needed replenishments anyway, so we resolved to kill two birds with one bottle of vodka from the town liquor store. When I told Tim—wine expert, president of the business association, and newly appointed West Nile Virus consultant—the story of the hawk, the raccoon, and the woodpile, he immediately took a few steps back and asked, "You didn't touch it, did you?"

"Not the raccoon," I said, "but Scott touched the hawk!"

"I didn't *touch* it," Scott said defensively like he'd just been accused of having the cooties. "I *shoveled* it." [He touched the hawk. I saw him. But if he wants to shovel it and say that he didn't touch it, we'll humor him. From a distance.]

"You're not supposed to even touch it with a shovel," Tim continued ominously. "You have to wash it with bleach or something. You better call Animal Control."

"Are they open on Saturday?"

"Or just call the state police," Tim finished.

By the time we got home, I had already decided that Scott would be the one to call the police, and I told him so. "I'll sound dumb," I begged off. "I'm nervous as it is."

We played a quick round of Rock Paper Scissors, and even though I lost, Scott called the police. He gave our number and a few details to a trooper who said he'd have someone call us back. To curb Jasper's curiosity, I went out and turned the wheelbarrow over on top of the masked bandit. While Jasper tried to get the raccoon to come out from under the wheelbarrow, Scott and I paced around, looking for further clues. "I hope they don't have to quarantine our yard." I said. "Immy is coming this week to plant the rose garden."

"Rose garden?!" Scott asked. Fortunately, the phone rang, saving me from a thorny discussion. It was Animal Control. I stood by as Scott explained the dead raccoon, and, at my insistence, he went through the *our house via Westchester* scenario. "Yes. No. No." Scott nodded and shook his head. "A little. About two feet."

My imagination ran wild hearing half a phone call.

"It was not two feet," I said in a conversation I wasn't having. "The raccoon was right where the hawk was!"

Scott covered the mouthpiece and hissed, "He is not asking where we found them. He's asking how deep I buried the hawk."

Oh.

Back to the conversation: "No. No. I can. Do I need to do anything special to the shovel? Um, like clean it? Oh. Uh huh. Okay. Thank you, sir."

"What did he say?" I fretted.

"Nothing to worry about," Scott surmised.

"Nothing to worry about?" I huffed. "Two dead animals in two weeks by one woodpile!"

"He said the bird was probably chasing a mouse and probably broke its neck by hitting the woodpile and the raccoon probably ate poison."

"Did you tell him that the only poison in our yard is ivy?"

"Stop worrying," Scott said way too matter-of-factly. "He said we should just bury the raccoon a little deeper than we buried the hawk."

So, that's what we did. We dug a very deep hole and, being experienced funeral directors, held a slightly more elaborate ceremony for the raccoon than we had for the hawk. And, being paranoid, I doused us both in *Deep Woods Off*.

13

THE PERGOLA PROJECT

When we'd finally finished the seventh coat of paint on the Zen room wall, Scott and I decided to take a few minutes to meditate among the fumes. I'm not sure what Scott spent his five minutes thinking about, but I spent mine focusing on the glob of paint that he had gotten on the floor and praying real hard for inner peace to accept it.

Once the urge to scream had passed, I went outside and found Immy out by the Jacuzzi putting the final touches on our new brick patio. She and Jim had made three trips north of Albany to score antique brick for us, and were just finishing several weeks of laying a gorgeous brick patio around the Jacuzzi.

"I love the old brick," I cooed. "The extra effort was definitely worth it! It looks like it's been here forever." And, as

Scott wrote out another check, I reminded him, "Aren't we lucky that they only charge for their time?"

The following week, the first rain fell on our new patio. "Oh, my God!" Immy shouted into our city answering machine. "Have you seen your bricks? I'd say at least two hundred of them have taken in moisture and... they've popped." As it turned out, quite a few of our antique bricks were "interior bricks." They were not made for direct exposure to the weather. So, Immy and Jim were back, replacing all the "exploding bricks" with new bricks they were aging with a paint wash that Immy had concocted. Soon the patio would once again be perfect.

Fortunately, they only charge for their time.

One night as Scott and I soaked beneath the stars, I had a vision. "A pergola over the patio would finish it off," I suggested.

"That'd be nice," Scott agreed. "Or we could just make an awning of dollar bills. Wouldn't that be pretty?"

"Pergolas aren't that expensive," I insisted and consciously chose to leave the conversation at that. The next day, I purchased a book titled *Outdoor Structures* and called Immy to get her up to speed on the idea. I described the many different styles that were possible, and suggested that I'd help Jim on the project. "That way," I said, "Scott will see that we're saving money and I'll get to learn some new skills."

I became a helper obsessed. I purchased four books, amassed *hundreds* of pictures of pergolas and arbors, and spent hours on the phone with Immy debating the merits of every column, board, curve, and angle. By the time we all got together in person to discuss the look of the thing, Jim finally had heard and seen enough. "Here's what we're going to do…" he said firmly, putting his hammer down and picking up a pencil. He drew out the structure and pointed at it. "That's the pergola," he said. I could tell by the way that he picked his hammer back up that he meant it.

Day one. Jim walked by me in the driveway bare-handedly carrying a sixteen-foot board as if it were a toothpick. I was straining to pick up one of the shorter boards. "Did Immy tell you the bad news?" he asked.

"What bad news?" I replied, deciding against the board and instead helping with the saw.

"About the glitch."

Immy got out of the car with a tray of coffee. "Well," she began, "we can't paint it. Pressure treated wood can't be painted or stained for at least three months."

"Three months?" I said. "I'm going to have to look at naked wood for three months?"

"I know," Immy said. "I can't believe I forgot that. Pressure treated has to dry out. Want some coffee?"

"Surely somebody in this county has *aged* pressure treated wood," I insisted, taking a cup of coffee.

While I sipped my coffee, I sat on the porch and called *every* lumber company in the county looking for pressure treated wood ready for painting, or at least trying to find someone who would tell me we could paint it right away: "Three months." "Six months." "I'd wait at least a year." Finally, I found an authoritative sounding fellow at Lowe's that gave me the answer I wanted to hear. "Painting pressure treated wood?" the guy repeated tentatively. "I'd wait two days."

I covered the mouthpiece. "Lowe's says two days!" I shouted to Immy and Jim.

Then, I heard a voice in the background at Lowe's yell: "Two months! Two months!"

"I'm sorry," my mis-informant said. "I meant two months."

I hung up the phone and moped over to Immy. "What is this?" I asked Immy. "Some kind of sicko lesson in patience."

"We'll paint it as soon as we can," Immy promised. "The man at the lumberyard said we could paint it when it passed the water test."

"What's the water test?" I said optimistically. "Maybe it'll pass it now."

"If you pour water on the wood and the water runs off," Immy said, "the wood's not ready to paint."

I grabbed a bottle of water, and we all headed to the stack of boards. I dumped water on the board, and it ran off faster than water down a duck's back. Then I poured water on another board. Same result. "It seems to me," I reasoned impatiently, "if water runs off, that's a good thing."

Immy smiled. "Um, that means the paint will run off too."

"Oh."

Construction begins. Had you been driving down our road the day the construction began on our pergola and happened to look across the creek, you might have noticed a kook dangling precariously on a ten-foot ladder in nothing but a towel. That would have been me. I had my phone in one hand and a tape measure in the other, and I was having one last "*where to position the columns*" conversation with Immy.

"I think if we place the center columns nine feet in," I calculated, "we'll still be able to see the fountain from the living room." I had insisted we create a fountain out of our old hand dug well. I got Scott to approve that project by telling him it would be bad karma to fill it in. When he suggested we just cover it, I quickly told him the story of little Timmy who fell down this well near my grandmother's house. That had done the trick. And after all that expense of making it into a fountain, I surely didn't want to have a pergola column blocking my view of it!

"Alright," Immy said, once again humoring me. "We'll be there in a little while, and I'll get Jim to hold up a column so you can check. Don't forget our new assistant is coming with us, and remember, he's shy." I got the hint—*don't scare him away on his first day*.

So the team was Jim, master planner; Immy, coffee, errands, lunch, and garden clean-up; Mr. Shy, Jim's new assistant; and me, slave labor.

When Immy, Jim, and Mr. Shy arrived with a truckload of supplies, Jim got out of the truck and immediately went over, and lifted a column into place. Immy and I proceeded to check the view of the fountain from every window in the house. After that was settled, the conversation turned to a lot of talk about "two-by-tens," "six-by-sixes," "deck screws," and "span." Then, "girth," "thickness," and "length."

"Ooooh," Mr. Shy said, uttering his first sound all day, "I'm unexpectedly interested."

Mr. Shy suddenly didn't seem so shy.

Eight hours later, Mr. Shy had dug six of the three-foot holes needed for our eight columns. Jim pulled down the driveway and got out of his truck in a huff. "We've got another glitch," he growled. "That dang store sold all of my six-by-sixes."

"What?" Immy said, letting go of a weed. "The ones we already paid for? Well, we'll never go there again."

"Now, what are we going to do?" I moaned.

"Time to go visit Homer," Jim said. He and Immy climbed in the truck and headed to Home Depot. Mr. Shy and I stayed back to finish the last two holes. While they were gone, I asked Mr. Shy what he did before he began helping Immy and Jim.

"I'm a female impersonator," he said as he stuck his shovel into the soil.

I dropped my hole-digger and my jaw. "*A what?!*" I asked.

"A drag queen. My name is *Holiday*. I do bachelor parties, telegrams, and club shows." By the time Immy and Jim's truck rumbled back down the driveway, Holiday had given me all the juicy details. And I couldn't wait to tell Immy.

I ran to the truck. "Guess what?" I said, breathing hard from the jaunt across the lawn.

"Oh no," Immy said. "Don't tell me another glitch."

"No!" I screamed. "Your assistant is a *drag queen*!"

"I know. I didn't tell you?"

"No!" I squealed. "You said he was shy."

That night I called Scott, who was down in the city showing property so we could afford The Pergola Project, to tell him about the day's events.

"Guess what?" I enthused.

"It's finished?" he asked excitedly.

"No..." I paused dramatically and bit my lower lip, "but a drag queen named Holiday dug all our holes."

"A drag queen?" Scott asked bewilderedly. "Was she wearing high heels?"

"No! But he uses a live python in his act. Well, he did until the thing escaped."

"Who does he do?"

"Cher. Tina. Madonna. All the one-namers."

"I can't believe Immy and Jim have a drag queen as an assistant," Scott said, laughing. "Only in the country, friends. Only in the country."

"I know, I know," I enthused. "More tomorrow. And don't forget to pack the checkbook."

The next day, we cemented in eight columns. There was suddenly no turning back—our pergola was finally becoming a reality. After Holiday left for the day, I suggested to Jim and Immy that we needed two more columns to finish off the ends, "so it doesn't look like a drive-thru." Jim winced, but agreed.

Holiday arrived the next day early, and I broke the news to him about the two new holes. He had just finished digging when Immy and Jim drove up with two more six-by-sixes. "No more holes!" he yelled. *"It's like a hooker's dream."* Mr. Shy had gone on vacation and been replaced by Holiday who had obviously decided The Pergola Project was *her* new show.

"Oh, give it to me harder!" she screamed as Jim hammered. "A little to the left," she instructed as he positioned a board. "Oh, that's it, Papi! I feel it now." Then, whenever someone picked up a screwdriver, she'd ask, "You gonna screw me?" Jim and I laughed every time, but if I had been wearing pearls, I would have clutched them.

The next day, we began climbing the ten-foot ladders with boards that Holiday announced were "as heavy as my make-up case." While she worked on her act, our mission was to attach the boards to the columns with very long bolts, thereby forming the frame.

By sunset, we had a structure. "It looks almost exactly like that pergola on page 94 in *Outdoor Structure*," I bragged to Scott. Immy and I set about designing what Jim called the "*hoop de doos*"—the decorative outcroppings from each board and the braces. We accomplished our task after much trial and error. Getting the right aesthetic effect was, as Holiday noted, "harder than walking in six-inch heels over a subway grate."

At the end of the sixth day, we were done. And it was beautiful. Naked, but beautiful.

The next weekend, I bragged to my friend Don that our pergola was built by a drag queen. "Oh yeah?" he said. "I can top that. The contractor who worked on my house got arrested for murder."

"Did he do it?" I asked.

"Yep."

"Well, my drag queen uses a pet python in her act."

14

THE CUSHION

Since we don't really cook, Scott and I figured out a way to encourage more culinary activity—we decided to spruce up the kitchen. It seemed to us a much easier project than continuing to paint.

Our old stove—the one that singed my eyebrow off—and I had made amends, and it was now the centerpiece of our kitchen, giving me a daily opportunity to remind Scott that he had wanted to ditch it. The Napanee Electrified Kitchenette from Cathouse Antiques held goodies from local markets, and the free refrigerator that Immy and Jim wrangled out of a house their son was remodeling was cooling fine. So, a kitchen "renovation" seemed like a no-brainer. In fact, if anything, it would be relatively simple. The walls and cabinets just needed a coat of paint and the window seat needed a nicely upholstered cushion.

I decided to hold off a bit on the painting—having inhaled enough fumes in the past few weeks to keep me flying high as a kite for a few more—and instead, tackle the cushioning task first. I'd seen a sign in the window of a fabric store in Kingston: "Foam cut to order," and I figured they'd at least be able to offer me a recommendation on who might make such a thing.

Since the shape of the window seat was odd—sort of a triangle with appendages—traditional measurements were impossible, so I decided to make a pattern of the shape. After searching the house for something big enough to cover the seat, I came across a blue painter's tarp I had stuffed irritably into a corner of the basement after the Zen room work.

I dragged the crinkly plastic sheet up the stairs, flattened it out as best as possible on the kitchen floor, and stared at the Jackson Pollack splatter painting from past projects. The tarp was filthy and not exactly big enough, but with a few cuts here and a little duct tape there, I made it work. Necessity *is* the mother of all invention.

With my accoutrements of window seat design, I headed into the fabric store and asked who could help craft my window seat. "We make cushions," the woman behind the counter said in her droll monotone voice.

"Great," I said. "What's the process?"

"Process?" she asked, as she re-wrapped some loose fabric around a cardboard tube.

"I mean, how do I go about getting a cushion made?"

"First, you pick out your fabric, then you take measurements, then..."

"Oh, I have a pattern," I said proudly, holding up the crumpled blue mass. "My seat is sort of an odd shape."

"Well, pick out your fabric," she said pointing to the room.

I turned to face a patterned jungle, hundreds of bolts of fabric stacked and piled floor to ceiling in every square foot of available space. I took a deep breath and dove in. There were stripes and solids and multi-grained polyesters. There were plaids and denims and leftovers from the seventies. There were checks and polka dots and faux furs. My eyes zigzagged faster than my grandmother's Singer.

I quickly ruled out faux furs—although the faux cow was tempting. Solids, I decided were a little too dull. The polka dots were dizzying and the denim was rodeo-ish. My eyes settled on a delicate plaid—a perfect match to the "Homespun" green we'd picked out to paint our kitchen.

I toted the roll back to the keeper of the scissors, laid it on the cutting table, and unfurled my taped-together, painter's tarp pattern. A small mushroom cloud of dust and debris poofed upwards.

"That's dirty!" she exclaimed, waving her scissors around in the air.

"Sorry," I apologized, "but it was all I could find."

She huffed, then began measuring and figuring, figuring and measuring. "How thick?" she asked without looking up.

"Pardon me?"

She spoke louder and emphasized each word, "How thick would you like it?"

Remembering Scott's only opinion on the window seat was that he didn't "want just a cheesy foam cushion," he wanted it to be *fluffy*, I said: "I like it thick." I added a hand gesture: "About like this."

"A two inch foam core wrapped in two layers of batting," she advised.

At that point the only batting I knew was from Little League, so I brought out my secret weapon: *The Home Decorator's Bible*, flipped to a picture of a cushion I liked, and pointed. "Would it look like that?" I asked.

"Yes." She pulled out a calculator, and for what seemed like five minutes she punched numbers. Then, she quoted the price of a sofa.

I choked. I quickly debated between going to the dentist or cushioning my kitchen. The teeth could wait. "Okay. Let's do it. When will it be ready?"

"In eight to ten weeks," she said matter-of-factly, as if that would be okay.

"Eight to ten weeks! I could build a house in eight to ten weeks…"

"I can do it in a week," peeped a small voice from behind a pile of fabric. The woman with the scissors and I turned to see the eager face of a redheaded woman who had obviously been listening to our cushion conversation. Charlie Brown's cute little redheaded girl had grown-up, and she was open for business.

"Eight weeks" or "One week." *Hmmmm? What to choose? What to choose?*

"You've got yourself a deal," I said to the grown-up cute little redheaded girl. The woman with the scissors was not a happy woman.

"I'm Bruce," I said to my seamstress-in-waiting.

"I'm Carla," she said, handing me her card. *Stone Ridge Upholstery—Pick up and delivery available.*

"Stone Ridge?" I said excitedly. "I live in Stone Ridge."

"What's your last name?" Carla asked.

"Littlefield." She stared at me. We were silent for a moment. "I'll call you later today," I said, gathering my *Decorator's Bible* and painter's tarp and heading for the door.

"How do you know she can make a cushion?" Scott asked when I recounted the story.

"She was in a fabric store buying fabric," I answered as if that were obvious.

"So were you," Scott reminded me.

"Oh. Well, I'll ask for references."

I called Carla to feel her out. "I'm so glad you called," she said. "As soon as you left the store I realized you were the Bruce that writes that column. Have you had any more run-ins with Jabba the Hutt?" I gulped. "Don't worry. I love your column. I only buy that paper each week so I can read your piece."

Forget references, I was sold. If she didn't know how to sew, at least she knew good writing. "Want to drop by for a cup of coffee tomorrow, so I can show you where the cushion is going to go?"

The following morning Carla came over. I had my makeshift pattern spread out on the window seat. "A little wrinkled," she said as she tried to smooth it out.

"It won't flatten," I told her. "Believe me, I tried. I will also tell you that ironing is out of the question. There's still a plastic coat of blue on my iron where I tried that. Would you like sugar with your coffee?"

"Yes," she said, not taking her eyes off her measuring. "Four."

"Four sugars?" I gasped. "No wonder you can do it in a week."

A day into her work, Carla called and asked if she could come take a few more measurements. Upon returning to the house, she walked into the kitchen and pulled out her tools. "Some of the angles didn't quite make sense," she said rather scientifically. A nice way of saying—*your blue pattern sucks.*

A few days later, Carla came down the driveway, pulled a huge cushion out of her van and lugged it into the house. "I said a week and I meant it," she said proudly as she put it in place.

"Wow!" I said. "It's perfect."

"You got the last two cans of Scotch Guard available," she told me triumphantly.

"Last two cans?" I asked.

"They've taken it off the market," she said. "Seems to be finding a way into people's bloodstreams." I smiled at the cushion and its matching pillows. "But if it gets dirty, just use a damp cloth and wipe it off."

"Oh, it won't get dirty," I said. "I'm going to put a plastic sheet over it just like my Aunt Jean's sofa!"

We both laughed, but after she left, I threw a sheet over the cushion. I needed to research the half-life of Scotch Guard.

15

FRENCH DOORS

We wanted to replace the sliding glass door that goes out to our Jacuzzi with French doors. Actually, it wasn't a sliding glass door at all. I referred to it as our "dragging glass door" because opening it was like rolling the rock away from The Tomb.

I was fixed on French doors, but finding a traditional wood pair was proving to be an impossible feat. I discovered that modern French doors have what are called "divided lights," which means the panes weren't individual glass panes, but instead, were wood grids affixed to the glass on each side of the door. I also found doors with "true divided lights," in which a laminated wood grid is imbedded within double panes of glass, but those still seemed a little too pre-fab for our old house.

I insisted we find the real deal—a pair of real French doors. After countless shopping expeditions in and out of antique stores, auctions, and even to a demolition yard, we finally came home with a pair from a Kingston junk shop owned by one of the infamous dueling brothers of junk—the Zelinsky's.

The brother named Barry runs a shop called "Dan'z," and the brother named Dan runs a shop called "Zelinsky's." Local legend has it that years ago the brothers had a tiff over a Lionel toy train set and never spoke again. But neither of them talks about the row. Barry kept Dan'z, and Dan moved into a big warehouse building that was once an old shirt factory. After visiting both operations numerous times, we finally found a pair of French doors at Dan'z that Barry sold us for a song.

I was jubilant as we drove home with them sticking out the back window of the Wagoneer. "See," I preached to Scott. "Patience *is* a virtue."

When we got home, I insisted that we take them out immediately and at least lean them against the dragging glass door "for appreciation value." After carrying them into the house (knocking over Scott's prized geranium in the process), we finally got them in place. It was then, when we stood back to admire their perfectness, that we noticed a *slight* problem.

"Why does the one on the left look different than the one on the right?" Scott asked as we curiously stared at the pair.

"Because they are different!" I said. "We don't have a pair of French doors. We've got a French door and a French door! How did we not see that?"

"What kind of return policy do you think they have at that junk shop?" Scott asked.

"Well, it's not 'Bloomingdale's.'"

We loaded the mismatched pair into the Wagoneer and headed back to Dan'z to see Barry. It was left to *me* to do the talking because as Scott explained: "Well, you did pick them out." I did. I admit it. I picked out the *first* one and Scott found us its "pair."

We found Barry standing beside a giant lion cage. I approached sheepishly. "Um, we have a problem..." I began in my most pitiful tone.

"What's up?" he asked.

"Well, the pair of French doors we bought isn't actually a pair after all."

"You can't make them work?" he urged.

"I don't think so," I said. "Unless we want our back patio to look like a funhouse at the fair."

"Okay, bring 'em in," he said. We leaned the doors against an old streetlamp, and he handed back our cash.

We left Dan'z happy. "Barry was really nice to give our money back," I said.

"Yep," Scott agreed. "But we're still stuck with the same dragging glass door."

A week later, I woke up on the wrong side of the bed—the side I couldn't get out of. Somewhere between "good night" and "good morning" my back had become as stiff as a beauty contestant's hair. "Scott," I yelped, "I can't move."

Already a couple of hours ahead of me in his day, Scott cheerily came into the room. "Your foot asleep?" he chirped.

"No. It's my back."

"Your back's asleep?" he drilled.

"No!!!" I howled, fixing my eyes involuntarily on the ceiling. "I-can't-move-my-back! *I'm stuck*!"

I thought perhaps I was having a nightmare. I soon learned that I was—a waking one. Scott slowly and gingerly lifted me off the bed to my *eeeks* and *iiikes*. I was the tin man before grease. My back was definitely *out*. Out-of-the-ballpark out.

"How'd you do that?" Scott questioned.

"I worked all night on it," I snapped. "I was fine when I went to sleep."

"Maybe you just slept on it wrong," he counseled.

"Did you ever think of med school?" I asked sarcastically.

After a trip down to New Jersey and Scott's chiropractor brother, it was diagnosed that while scurrying in and out to the patio with drinks and hors d'oeuvres for visiting friends the night before, I had yanked too many times on the dragging glass door. Now, the bane of my existence had become the breaker of my back.

Scott had to get back to the city on business, and I had to stay in the country—alone in my agony—to deal with house projects, and at some point, get some writing done.

I spent the next few days a *stiff-back-about-town*, moaning pathetically to anyone who would listen and vying for the sympathy vote. "You look like you're in pain," Sue, our local bank manager noted, as I slumped into her office chair.

"I am." After a brief discussion of the advantages of Midol, Sue felt Motrin might suit me better and handed over three "to get you started." I'm not normally a pill popper, but I threw them back with nothing but a gulp of saliva. After an hour of refinancing paperwork, a slight smile had grown on my face.

Maybe it was the Motrin, or it could have been that the new percentage rate was going to save us over a hundred thousand dollars over the life of our loan.

Heavily anesthetized, I drove home. As I passed the town park, I had an idea. My dad hangs upside down from gravity boots to release his back pain. Dressed in slacks and a linen shirt, I meandered over to the jungle gym as inconspicuously as possible and took off my shoes. I climbed up the wood and steel structure, and threw my legs over a monkey bar.

In one fell swoop, I dove backwards and was dangling by bent knees. My dress shirt flapped over my head, and I struggled to tuck it back in to hide my belly. I suddenly noticed the upside down world around me. Less than fifty feet away, an adult softball team had stopped their game and the players were all gawking at me. I gave a meek wave to the pitcher.

When I climbed off the equipment, I covered my face and walked back to the car. I might have been embarrassed, but my back did feel better.

16

POISON IVY

Shortly after sunrise on one of the last remaining mornings of our first country summer, I wiped my blurry eyes and looked out the window to see Scott down on the banks of the creek dramatically fighting with the jungle of vines about to overtake our "beach." Jasper and I exchanged our usual morning "hellos"—his, a tired lick, and mine, a tired scratch. I staggered toward the aroma of coffee wafting up the stairs from the kitchen.

With my first sip came a sudden and terrifying realization. Barefoot, I sprinted out of the house and down the lawn. "Wait!" I yelled to Scott. "Stop!" At the bottom of the hill, I came upon an awful scene: Scott—dirty, soiled, and shirtless—standing proudly beside a pile of twisted vine and greenery the size of a large buffalo. "I think there's poison ivy in there!"

"Calm down," he said. "I'll take a shower in a little while."

"I think you should wash it off *now*," I implored. Having grown up in the South, poison ivy and oak were words of panic to me. The neighbor kid had been hospitalized from it.

"I will when I'm *finished*," he said through clenched teeth. "Why can't you just say 'good job,' instead of nagging?"

I looked at the cleared beach and then back to the twisted mound of vine. "It looks great!" I congratulated. "But I'm counting a lot of leaves-of-three in that pile. I don't want you to have to spend our entire time in Key West miserable."

"I'll wash with the Tecnu Immy left us in a little while," he said.

"Alright, but I'm just warning you," I said ominously, "if you have it on your hands, it'll spread to wherever you touch."

"Ooooh," he moaned walking towards me with his arms outstretched like a zombie. *"Poy-zun iiii-veeeee. Hah. Hah. Hah."*

Two days later, we were on a plane to Key West when I noticed Scott itching his forearm. "What'cha scratchin'?" I asked sadistically.

"I've got a couple of mosquito bites."

"Hmmmm." I nodded and quickly averted my suspicions to the pages of *Sky Mall*.

We arrived at the resort and hurriedly changed into our bathing suits to catch one of Key West's glorious sunsets. "What's that on your back?" I questioned, as Scott bent over to slip on his flip-flops.

"I have a little poison ivy," he admitted in a most pitiful schoolboy voice. I squeezed my lips together tightly to avoid a cruel giggle.

While strolling down Duval Street, my peripheral vision caught peeks of Scott's persistent body part patting. Evil Ivy was setting in faster than the sunset.

By the following morning, Scott had poison ivy in a variety of venues, including some quite interesting cracks and crevices. "Remember when I said *wherever* you scratched, it would spread?" I asked, in an admittedly told-you-so tone.

"Shut-up," he told me.

While I sat by the pool and applied my coconutty suntan lotion, Scott applied the medicinally scented cortisone he had just picked up at the hotel convenience store. Scott's mother, who had graciously taken the entire family on the trip, pointed at Scott's leg and asked rather dramatically, "What is *that*?"

Scott looked at me, then back at his mother. "It's poison ivy."

"Oh, you *bettuh* not touch the *bay-be*," she warned. "That stuff is high-*lee* contagious."

Scott's itching and scratching became the comic relief of our vacation, but I must admit that he was a poison ivy trooper. He went bar hopping—and did some stool top scratching. He went snorkeling—and did some underwater scratching. He went parasailing—and proved that he could even scratch a couple hundred feet in the air.

Getting back from Key West was about as difficult as getting rid of Scott's poison ivy. Our flight from Key West to Miami had mechanical problems and we, along with seventeen other irate passengers, were packed into a mini-bus bound for Miami on a mission to make our connecting flights. The mini-bus flew down the two-lane road, pushing the speed and its passengers' stomachs to the limit. Throughout the journey, I had to keep reminding Scott to keep his *contagion* leg on his side of the seat and away from my ivy-free one.

In order to try and make the four-hour road trip in less than three and a half hours, it was announced that we wouldn't be stopping for any bathroom breaks, and there wasn't one on board. Two hours outside of Miami, a woman stood up and asked the busload of her fellow passengers if it would be all right to stop. A high-haired, hardhearted woman from Baltimore yelled back, "No! I have to make my plane."

"Do you feel like we're on *Survivor?*" I whispered to Scott.

One hour outside of Miami, the woman who needed to stop stood back up waving a diaper in the air. "I have a bladder problem," she groaned. "I'm willing to go in the diaper if someone will let me have a private seat."

"Stop the bus!" we all began to yell, except Ms. Baltimore, who was looking around to see if there was an empty seat.

"I've got to pitch this idea to CBS," I told Scott as we sat outside a Burger King waiting for *Pampers* to finish her business. "Can't you see it? Nineteen people stuck on a bus headed across country..."

"Shhh!" Scott said as he scratched.

We made it to Miami just after our plane's scheduled departure, but because of a delay, we were allowed on the flight. After a lengthy sit—giving me plenty of time to once again consider the toilet paper iPod docking station in *Sky Mall*—the pilot came on and announced that due to a storm along the east coast, our flight to Newark wouldn't be leaving until "at least ten o'clock." Given that it was eight, they reopened the plane, and we were all let off to roam the Miami Airport.

At ten, we all re-boarded and the plane prepared for push-back. *Whawawaw. Whooop! Whawawaw.* We all sat in a suddenly darkened plane.

When the lights came back on, the captain announced calmly, "Folks, nothing to worry about. While at the gate we were hooked up to an extension cord type thing to give us power. When they unhooked us our independent power had a momentary failure, but everything is fine. We have one engine running." Panic ensued. Spanish was being tossed like a salad and a few people began to cross themselves. An Erik Estrada look-alike and his posse stormed the front, banging on the cockpit door. We had a mutiny on our hands.

"Folks," the captain said on the intercom, "it seems there are some passengers who want off this flight and, even though I've explained that nothing is wrong, federal regulations require that we allow them off. Our flight attendants have now been on duty too long and if we open the plane, they will need to end their service today. This flight will have to be cancelled." All out chaos broke out.

The worried passengers got off, the flight attendants stayed to a hero's salute, and we finally landed in Newark at three a.m. Scott and I took the shuttle bus to the far reaches of civilization, known as "long term parking," and climbed into the Wagoneer. I turned the key. Nothing. I turned the key again. Nothing. I turned to Scott. "Nothing."

Upon further inspection, we found that Scott had left his reading light on. For six days while we were having fun in the sun, the little light was draining the Wagoneer's big battery. Scott scratched his head. For a brief moment, I was glad he itched. Then, I felt bad for him and worse for our situation. "What are we going to do?" I asked as we sat in a dark car.

"I'll call our tow service," Scott said. Luckily, while Scott was on the phone, he noticed a guy getting into a pick-up and asked if he had jumper cables. He did, and by 4:20 a.m., through the kindness of a stranger, we were finally home.

17

THE BUZZ

"Okay," the stunning waitress said as she poured Scott and me coffee early one Saturday morning at the Nibble Nook. "My name's Maggie. I'm a fan of your column, and I want to know something."

"What's that?" I asked.

"Where can I get some Tecnu?"

"At the drugstore," Scott said, putting down his fork and scratching the remaining remnants of his rash.

"Or," I suggested, "why don't you come by our house, and we'll give you some?" I had bought a few extra bottles of it in case there was ever a Scotch Guard type ban on it.

"That'd be great," she said as I took a bite of my eggs. "My stepfather has some stuff I can bring over about the old bungalow colony that was at your house. It was like *Dirty Dancing*, you know? And I'd love for you to see my mom's garden." We decided that Maggie would come by the next day for her bottle of Tecnu, and then we'd drive to her mom's, where we would drool over her garden.

The following afternoon, Maggie rumbled down our drive in her big black Suburban, got out, and opened the back doors. Inside was a piece of Eden. "I thought I'd bring you some plants," she laughed as we all stared at the 4x4 jungle. "Do you think you can use 'em?"

"We can always use plants," I said, greedily pulling them out of the truck and choreographing their placement around the yard. After a quick tour around Edgewater and a look at our now infamous pergola, Scott, Maggie, and I jumped in her Suburban and headed up the road for a look at her mother's gardens.

Walking around her mom's home was like flipping through *House Beautiful*. "My uncle's an interior designer," Maggie explained proudly as we toured about, "and he and my mother like to play." Everything—from draperies to art to hostas—was perfect, but we found the greatest treasure tucked upstairs in a small reading room. Maggie gently touched the shoulder of an elegant woman in her 90's. "Me-Maw?" she said. "These are my friends, Scott and Bruce."

The woman looked up from her book, her face dappled with warm afternoon light. "Nice to meet you," she smiled.

"What'cha reading?" I asked. Her delicate hand lifted *Fried Green Tomatoes* for examination.

"Cool. Fanny Flag is funny! Isn't she?"

Me-Maw lit up like a schoolgirl who'd just been asked to the school dance. "I love her humor," she said.

"Bruce is a writer, Me-Maw," Maggie told her great-grandmother.

"Oh," she nodded, "I love to read. That's what I like to do now, is read."

We all talked to Me-Maw for a while, her great-grandmother watching me carefully. When Maggie said it was time for us to go, Me-Maw turned her head, looked at me with her gentle eyes, and exclaimed, "You're so handsome and full of life!"

Me-Maw's schoolgirl flirtation left a smile on my face, and her heartfelt sincerity fertilized my soul.

A few days later, Maggie showed up at my door with a pie. "Me-Maw can't stop talking about you," she said with a smile. "We made pies this afternoon, and she wanted me to bring you one."

"That makes my day," I said. "Tell her I think she's a beauty through and through." While Jasper investigated the smell of Maggie's creation, our newest contractor, Harry, hammered and drilled in the background. We had at long last found a matching pair of antique French doors and installing them was on Harry's lengthy To Do list.

"Mine!" I barked to Jasper. I placed the pie on the kitchen table. There was a noticeable vibration in the ceiling above. "Do you hear that?" I asked Maggie.

"Yeah," she said, pointing up at the ceiling.

I stood on a chair with the intention of tapping the ceiling to hush what I assumed to be a buzzing pipe. My fingers poked through the ceiling as if it were paper, and bees spilled from the hole like candy out of a piñata. Maggie and I simultaneously shrieked. "*AAAAAAAH*! AAAAAAH!" Were we auditioning for horror film scream queens, we would have definitely been cast.

During our escape to the safety of outside, Maggie lost one of her shoes. "HARRY!" I yelled as I frantically searched for the hornet spray among the plethora of poisons beneath the garden cart on the backporch. "HARRY! HELP! WE NEED HELP!"

Harry left the French door project and came running. Well, Harry is as steady as he goes, so I wouldn't say he came running—I'd say he came walking. I traded him the bug spray for his hammer, and he bravely went into the line of fire.

Maggie and I watched the scene from the other side of the kitchen window screen. Harry was blasting bee killer and Jasper, surrounded by the cloud of bees, was stoicly guarding Maggie's pie. "What's that mint smell?" Maggie asked.

Uh, oh. In my frenzy, instead of grabbing the "Wasp and Hornet Killer that kills on contact with a 22-foot jet spray," I'd given Harry the "Fresh Mint Scented Poison Free Ant & Roach Killer"—the can *with the pictures of the ant and cockroach on the label.* I ran around and opened the gardener's bench. I quickly snatched the can with the yellow jacket on the front and ran back to the kitchen.

By this time, Harry had realized that the fresh mint scent was more like a yellow jacket anesthetic. Instead of an instantaneous nosedive, the Ant & Roach Killer caused a slow, sputtering demise for yellow jackets, which makes them *really* angry. But, after ten minutes of buzzing chaos, Harry had the situation under control. Maggie found her other shoe, Jasper had successfully protected the pie, and Harry—our humble Unstung Hero—went back to installing the door.

On a positive note, the Ant & Roach killer did leave the kitchen with a fresh minty scent for days.

18

DE PINK CHAIRS

Before we owned a country house, we never had to fix a broken oven, remedy a clogged toilet, or worry whether there was oil for heat. New York City apartments do have broken ovens, clogged toilets, and need heat, but in a city apartment these tasks are cured by a crack-flashing group of professionals known as "Superintendents."

We love our super Leopoldo. He and his wife, Isabella, are from Guatemala, and, one day soon, after making their much-deserved American fortune, they hope to return to Guatemala and tend to their coffee bean farm. In order to hurry along The Guatemalan-American Dream, Isabella took a job as the housekeeper to a wealthy English couple, and in addition to her weekday job with them in the city, Leopoldo and Isabella spent their weekends upstate caring for the English couple's country home in our neighboring town.

A few years back, the Englishwoman's health deteriorated due to Parkinson's disease, and they decided to return to their mother country, quickly selling their Manhattan apartment and their country home for top dollar and leaving for England. Isabella's last task of employment was emptying the upstate house of all its furnishings and preparing it for sale to the new owners.

A few days before the house was set to close, Scott and I arrived in the country for the weekend to a series of increasingly desperate messages on our answering machine.

Message one: "Bruce, dis is Isabella. Wheeel you call me?" Then she left her cell phone number.

Message two: "Bruce, dis Isabella. I need give you furniture. Pleeeeeeze, you come over." She left a different cell phone number and an address.

Message three: "Bruce, dis is your freeend Leopoldo. My wife needs you help her. She wants you have furniture. Today. Thank you." He gave yet another number.

A friend in need is a friend in deed, especially if they have furniture to give away! I left messages on each of the three phone numbers that we were coming over, and Scott and I jumped in the car heading toward the Spanglished address Isabella had left on the machine. We journeyed south on Route 32, keeping our eyes peeled.

"Hey," Scott pointed. "There's Isabella!" I looked in my rear view window to see our super's short wife jumping up and down alongside the road. I did a quick u-turn and pulled up next to Isabella.

"I give you furniture!" she yelled as I rolled down my window. "*Free*!"

Right as we were about to get out of the car, Scott, in typical Scott fashion, turned to me and said, "I don't want us going home with a whole lot of stuff. I know how you are at these kinds of things."

"Alright," I promised, smartly hiding my contempt. "But free is free."

We walked onto the house's wraparound porch and found Leopoldo in a sweat. I gave him a *we're-out-of-the-city* hug and immediately became entangled in a "You want?-You take!" tango, a dance between diverse tastes—Leopoldo's, Scott's and mine.

Proving that one man's trash is another man's treasure, Leopoldo would point to something new, and I'd point to something old. He, for example, couldn't believe I wanted the dusty box from the basement that said "Lipton's Coffee 1904," but didn't want the bathroom's brand new wicker mirror from Wal-Mart.

Scott wouldn't know how to spot a treasure, even if it had an X on it. He, for example, turned his nose up at an inlaid table I was caressing. I shot him a dirty look, and quickly asked Leopoldo, "Is this table available?"

"You want?" Leopoldo asked, again rather surprised at my taste. "You take!" He pointed to a pair of chocolate brown La-Z-Boy recliners, "You take, too."

"I never sit down Leopoldo," I said truthfully. "You should have them."

By dusk, Scott and our Grand Wagoneer had reached their limit. "Enough!" he insisted.

"There's a lot more," I said. "We haven't even made a dent." I pointed to a 1950s medical cabinet in the kitchen. "I mean, look! That'd be perfect for 'Butch.'" [Butch is written on the side of a kid's camp trunk I'd bought at an auction. I fought a lesbian for it, and then decorated our guest room around it. When you stay with us, you feel like a spunky eleven-year-old.]

"Okay," Scott succumbed. "But that's it."

"What we do with all de rest of dis stuff?" Isabella asked, more like pleaded. Scott shivered in the corner while I catalogued the remaining Broyhill sofas, giant bookshelves, the pair of pink chairs, the pair of La-Z-Boys, miscellaneous lamps, and a complete wicker bedroom set that I'm sure was once fondled by Janice on the *Price is Right*. "Can we keep some of dees t'ings at your house?" I could see through a quick side eye that Scott was shaking his head.

"Well, we have a little room…" I said.

"…for a few boxes," Scott said, interrupting.

I momentarily debated throwing money on the floor for our "free" furniture and running, but I knew I'd have to see Isabella and Leopoldo again. "You know," I said, figuring it out as I talked, "I might… be able… to… sell the stuff that's left and make you some money."

"By dis Dursday morning?" Isabella asked anxiously.

"What time?" I asked, grimacing.

"8:30."

I nodded my head. Unknowingly, I had dug my grave and placed one foot on a banana peel.

Scott and I sat in stunned silence as we drove home. We had a floor lamp sticking out of the window, deck chairs tied off the back, a few things strapped to the roof, and an assortment of gardening tools in our laps. I was Sanford. He was Son.

It was Scott who finally broke the silence. "How in the heck are you going to get rid of the rest of that stuff by Thursday morning for cash?" he asked.

"One word: Immy." Something hanging off the car clanged its approval against the roof.

Early Wednesday morning, I drove up from the city, met Immy and her truck at the gas station, and together, we drove to meet Leopoldo at the furniture-filled farmhouse. The plan was that Immy would get some wicker furniture for her screened porch, and then the rest we'd sell to a friend of a friend of hers who owned a junk shop.

When we arrived at the house, it quickly became obvious that in addition to selling the furniture, Leopoldo also expected for me to be his co-mover. While Immy picked out some things for herself, Leopoldo and I dragged, shoved, and shimmied all the remaining items from the house onto the wraparound porch.

After Leopoldo and I carried out the final two pink chairs and collapsed on them, Immy called the junk dealer. When he arrived minutes later, he climbed up the porch stairs huffing and puffing his cigarette. I instantly recognized him as the chain smoker from a shop I frequented. He walked around appraising and fondling the merchandise as if he was at a Christie's pre-auction.

"What d'ya want for all of it?" he smiled, as he lit a cigarette with his cigarette. I hate this kind of negotiation, the one when I'm the seller not the buyer. Do you name the honest price you'll take or do you start with some inflated price in order to negotiate down? Immy fluttered five fingers behind Mr. Junk's head. His deal-making right eye caught her wave, and he laughed. "Oh, I could never spend that. How about three?"

He was either getting it for "three" or Leopoldo, Immy and me were going to be riding around the county selling off several truckloads of stuff one piece at a time. "Fine!" I readily agreed.

"$225 now," he added, "And $75 when you and her bring a load over to my shop."

Okay, fine. Shortly after the deal was done, Leopoldo announced he "needed to get back to the city," and asked if we'd take care of the rest. I suddenly realized that I had "sucker" written across my forehead. Fortunately, so did Immy.

At 9:20 that night, the ordeal was almost over. Immy and I had the last load of the day—the things going to our two houses—heaped on her truck. I was thanking her profusely for helping me when my cell phone rang. "*Brrroooooos?*" the voice on the other end said.

"Yes?"

"Dis Isabella. My huzbunnd make bad mistake. Where are de *peenk chairs?*"

"I sold them!" I announced proudly. "I'll give you the money tomorrow."

"I no want money. I need de peenk chairs," she said on the verge of hysterics.

"They're sold, Isabella!"

"No. Dey can't be sold! *Dey're in de contract*!"

I momentarily pulled the phone from my ear and turned white-faced to Immy: "You're not going to believe this."

"NO!!!!! I NEED DE PEENK CHAIRS!" my handset was screaming.

"Isabella. Calm down," I urged.

"DE PEE, PEE, PEEENK CHAIRS," she sobbed.

"I'll take care of it!" I hung up, and finally understood the meaning of "Finder's Keepers. Loser's Weepers." I was the loser.

"My life sucks," I whined to Immy as I waved goodbye out my car window and peeled off down her long driveway. I had to find *de peenk chairs* and get them back to the house before the following morning at 8:30 a.m. Using some research skills, I located the junk dealer's home phone number. When I called he seemed to barely remember me. He was either playing coy or had knocked back a few cocktails.

"I need to get back those pink chairs," I said frenziedly.

"Alright," he said. "A buck twenty-five for the pair."

"I'll pay, but I have to do it at 7:30 in the morning."

Fine. After we hung up I realized that I couldn't fit both pink chairs in my car, so I called Leopoldo and told him to meet me at the gas station near the house at 7:30 a.m. I was seriously ready to take care of this whole Lucy and Ethel mess. I also told him to tell his wife that there was now no need to jump from the George Washington Bridge.

The following morning proved continued chaos. I waited for Leopoldo until 8:30. He never showed. I went to the junk shop, handed over the cash for a pair of worn-out pink chairs, and told my junk friend to expect Leopoldo to come by and pick them up.

When I got home, there was a desperate message on my machine: "Broooos, you know de blue sofa…"

Don't ask. Just be thankful I didn't ask you to come look at my friend's free furniture.

19

WILDLIFE

"*Poop*!" I squeaked, a shiver running up my spine. "It's all over the top of the refrigerator and around the candy bowl!"

The week before, I came to the country to get some writing done and noticed our bowl of treats on the kitchen counter had been drastically depleted. Blaming first Scott, then Jasper as the sweet-toothed bandit, my latest discovery proved the culprit was a bit smaller in size, but just as crafty.

I called Scott to let him know the tiny rodents had launched a full-scale invasion on our home, even going so far as to fashion a fresh pinapple into a mini tropical condo. Next, I did what came naturally and called someone who could offer some actual advice for dealing with our squatting pests.

"Immy," I said, "I think we have mice! There are little black doo doos everywhere."

"Well, you can put out poison," she said. "But with Jasper you have to put it where he can't get it."

"What will happen to the mice?" I asked naively.

"They'll eat it and almost immediately get very thirsty. The idea is they'll leave the house searching for water."

"Then what?"

"*They'll die*," she whispered.

I thought of the sweet singing mice in the movie *Babe*. "I can't *kill* them," I moaned. "Mice are cute. Isn't there something else I can do?"

"Yes. They can live with you."

I called Cat House Antiques to get Bev's take on the matter. "What's your advice for mice?" I asked.

"Get a cat," she laughed. "Jasper likes cats."

"Yes, but can you see us driving back and forth from the city with a dog and a cat?"

"Good point," she said. "Well, Bill has these little traps."

"I can't stand the thought of snapping the heads off mice," I told her.

"These are the humane kind. Come on over. He'll show you."

Bev's husband Bill showed me a little plastic box that looked like a garage for a Matchbox car. "These things are great," he explained as he demonstrated. "You put a little piece of cheese in here. The mouse goes in. The door closes, and it's trapped. You can then take it outside and release it, or let it die and throw the box away."

I could see myself repeating this process over and over again. Cheese. *Squeak*. Release. Cheese. *Squeak*. Release. Or a worse and more likely scenario—coming home to little plastic coffins scattered all over our house. *There has to be something less mean*, I thought. I stalled.

The next weekend, we arrived in the country with friends who would be seeing the house for the first time. Scott impressed us all with a delicious waffle breakfast, and I gathered the dirty plates and took my position as Official Dish Washer. I began scrubbing, turning to talk to our friends who were still sitting around the kitchen table.

Suddenly, my head spun around faster than a rinse cycle in a Kenmore to address movement in front of me—"A mouse!" I shrieked. I ran across the kitchen and jumped on a chair. During my shriek-run-and-climb the mouse had pulled a Houdini, but I was still screaming. And standing on a chair.

I had always wondered why women in movies jumped on chairs when confronted with a mouse. As everyone laughed at me, I couldn't explain why I sought higher ground. Being elevated just felt safer, and it took a while for them to coax me down.

An all-out mouse hunt began. In the end we found no mice, but we did find Jasper's food stashed all over the house—kibble in the tub, in the stove, and in the cushions of our newly replaced sofas. And then, that night as I slipped my barefeet beneath the covers on my side of the bed, my toes met a stockpile of kibble! I ripped back the covers to find the sheets dotted with doo. "PREPARE TO DIE!!!" I announced.

The following morning, I headed out to buy Immy's poison and Bill's traps. The mice were going to meet their maker! Luckily for the mice, I had to stop to buy a trunk load of toilet paper at Sam's Wholesale Club—you know the place where everything really isn't cheaper, you just get more of it… without bags.

On my walk to Toilet Paper Mountain, there was an in-store demonstrator hawking a gadget that caught my ear: "…repels mice, spiders, and other nuisances with ultrasound." I walked over. "Won't harm cats and dogs. Not recommended for hamsters, guinea pigs, and rodent pets. Each covers up to 2000 square feet."

"I'll take four!"

I got home and pulled the palm-sized speaker with a luminescent nightlight from its packaging. "What if it makes Jasper neurotic?" Scott asked.

"Watch Jasper's face when I plug it in," I suggested. "If he starts twitching or anything, we'll take them back."

"Okay," Scott agreed.

"Wait a minute," I said, deciding to momentarily halt the operation. "What if I plug it in and mice run everywhere?" For good measure, I got a chair, stood on it, and plugged the Repeller in. Nothing. Not a creature stirred—not even a mouse. We placed the other three Repellers in strategic locations throughout the house, and that night I slept with one eye open as our tiny houseguests packed their bags.

On the Repeller's website I left my own testimonial: "I am proud to say that I can leave a piece of cheese on the counter overnight, and it will be there in the morning. Un-nibbled. I actually tried this, and we are mice free!" Somewhere, along the banks of the Esopus Creek, there is a whole colony of mice dwindling down their supply of kibble and asking themselves, "What the heck was that noise?"

20

TALKING TURKEY

As the leaves fell, the thought of Thanksgiving dinner hit me harder than the Pilgrim's first winter. Normally, Thanksgiving is no big deal—we'd walk to the diner a block up from our apartment and enjoy their blessed bounty. This year, however, we had a house. Scott's mother, as well as my brother and his new fiancé, had made a reservation for Thanksgiving at Edgewater Farm, and they would all be expecting a Martha Littlefield Stewart Thanksgiving feast.

I became panic-stricken and felt the need to begin asking everyone we encountered, "Do you know where we can get Thanksgiving dinner?"

"Oh, you can make a turkey," our friend Laurel encouraged. "It's so easy." This is a woman with olive oil for blood. Does she not remember how I singed off half an eyebrow trying to light my oven? Besides, what do I know about turkey? I'm the one who once asked my grandmother whether leaving a turkey in the freezer for a long time meant it would take longer to defrost. And let's get real. The thought of sticking my hands up into the inner sanctum of a bird sent shivers down my spine.

Scott chimed in. "We want to have Thanksgiving dinner at home," he said. "And a turkey won't fit in our oven."

"A turkey'll fit in your oven," she said, laughing. She should know—the last time our oven was used, she had made *us* dinner at *our* house."

"Okay, WE CAN'T COOK," I admitted. "There. I said it."

While the calendar crept toward the fourth Thursday of November, Scott and I were talking turkey to everyone we knew. Fortunately, the Pilgrims were watching over us. Maggie came by to pick up her pie plate. "What's that smell?" she asked, taking a big sniff in our kitchen.

"Rotting bee carcasses," I said, pointing to the taped up ceiling that had become coffin to thousands of yellow jackets.

"Eewww," she gagged. "That's so *gross*."

"I know. We're waiting until after Thanksgiving to get our ceiling redone."

"Oh, Thanksgiving!" Scott said, jumping at another opportunity to talk turkey. "Maggie, do you know anybody who'll make our Thanksgiving dinner?"

"How about Ivan's?" Maggie suggested. "They do a delicious dinner. I'll call them as soon as I get home." Thanks to Maggie, within an hour of her departure, the dinner deal was done.

"How big a bird do you want?" the nice woman on the phone asked as I confirmed the menu.

I shaped my hands into the size of the Butterball we always had growing up. "How big is a Butterball?" I asked.

"A fourteen-pounder should do you," she said, saving me from further humiliation.

"That'll be perfect!" I agreed, as if I knew my birds. "Now, what all comes with that?"

"Let's see," she said. "Cream of broccoli soup, stuffing, gravy, mashed potatoes, sweet potatoes, turnips, coleslaw, peas, cranberry sauce, rolls…" she stopped for a breath, then finished: "and an apple pie."

"A whole apple pie?!" Scott slobbered.

"That's what she said."

We could hardly wait for Thanksgiving and our *homemade* Ivan's feast.

We got up early Thanksgiving morning, feeling thankful that someone else had his hand up our turkey's butt. It was sunny and cold—in fact, it was one of the coldest mornings we had experienced in the country. "Let's get in the hot tub," I suggested. So, like two naked-mole rats, we scampered through the living room and out our new French doors.

"Don't close the…" I yelled one moment too late. The door closed and locked us out. "Oh well," I said, quickly shriveling, but remaining unusually calm. "We'll just go around to the front door when we get out." I tiptoed over to the hot tub, threw back the top, and climbed in.

"Dangit Scott!" I said, my cheerfulness chilled. "You turned off the hot tub last week instead of the fountain!"

"Oops," he said. "Okay, no hot tub. I'll run around and open the door."

While Scott streaked to the front of the house, I stood like a plucked turkey on the back lawn. "Happy Thanksgiving!" I said, waving across the creek to the cars driving by. Scott was desperately trying to use the hidden key to get in the door. "Did you deadbolt the door last night from the inside?" I hollered.

"Yep."

"Well, you'll have to crawl through the basement!" As Scott crawled through our dark, frightening basement, I hid behind a tree and shivered.

When my brother, Brian, and sister-in-law-to-be, Sandra, arrived at our house Thanksgiving Day, we gave them the grand tour. "Did you have any vegetables?" Brian asked as he looked at the frosted remains of our little vegetable garden.

"Sure," I boasted as we crunched through the patch. "Look, Scott! Our Brussels sprouts are finally ready." I nipped one and ate it. "Yum!"

"We'll add these to our *homemade* Thanksgiving dinner," Scott said, winking at me.

Both Sandra and Brian turned up their noses. "We hate Brussels sprouts," Brian said.

"Don't worry. We've *made* plenty of other stuff."

It was Scott's mother who, while sipping her second glass of pinot grigio, revealed we had "ordered out" our Thanksgiving dinner. She wasn't complaining. She was proud of our ingenuity. (She hasn't made a meal of her own since 1973.) "Why spend all that time in the kitchen, when you can spend it with your family?" she said.

While driving to Ivan's, all I could do was pray that our Thanksgiving dinner would be good. My brother and Sandra had driven fourteen hours for our fourteen-pound turkey.

"My stomach is growling," Scott said. "I hope we're going to have enough."

Minutes later, we were driving home with a bounty of boxes and a bird that was heavier than a bowling ball.

Since Scott's mother had given away our home cooking secret, we "cooked" in the open, which is to say, we dumped all the fixings in our decorative bowls, steamed our handful of Brussels sprouts, and went to the table. Scott carved the fourteen-pounder like a pro, and after a champagne toast, our ordered-in Thanksgiving dinner began.

"Keep your eye off that turkey dressing," my brother said.

"Why?" I asked.

"It makes him blush!"

21

OH, CHRISTMAS TREE

When I told Scott that Immy was taking me to pick out our Christmas tree before he'd be able to get to the country, he readily relinquished the duty. "That's okay," he said rather happily. "You and Immy go. You'll have fun." I knew exactly what he was thinking—*poor Immy*. He hates being near me for the little choices in life. The big ones—buying a house, buying a car—I do on impulse, but the little ones overwhelm me. When making those types of decisions, I often suck in and suck the life out of everyone within my vicinity.

Picking a Christmas tree in the city each year had become a relatively painless endeavor. A routine makes it safe. Between dog walk and dinner, we rush to the local Korean deli I call "Kim's Mark-Up" and quickly peruse the imported forest Mr. Kim has leaning against makeshift wooden supports. Since he only has about a dozen specimens, the choice isn't too difficult.

There are usually a couple of shorties for those people living in closets. We can move past those. There's also the obligatory Green Giant for the neighborhood fashion editor with fourteen-foot ceilings. Though tempting, Green Giant would have to bend in half in order to fit in our apartment. What's left is a handful of average trees. After an attempted haggle over price (Mr. Kim never budges), we walk a block home toting our tree over our shoulders.

This year, since we had a house in the country, I decided it was time to start a new tradition—perhaps at the ShopRite or the Home Depot. And that's what we'd planned to do, until I got a call from Immy. "We're going Friday to get a tree," she said. "Do you want to go with us?" I figured we'd go to ShopRite or Home Depot together, pick out our trees, and she'd help me lug mine back to Edgewater Farm in the back of her truck.

When we firmed up plans, I learned we were going to a tree farm where we would pick and cut a tree ourselves. It was to be a family outing with Immy, her husband Jim, their daughter Kathy, grandson Jimmy, and my furry sidekick Jasper. Among us we had six trees to buy. I'm sure you've already figured out whose took the longest and caused the most drama, but I'll tell you the story anyway.

I stepped out of the truck at Marshall's Tree Farm and was faced with more Christmas trees than I had ever seen in my life. The tree farmer, Mr. Marshall, welcomed us by giving us a saw. I instantly saw one thing: I was headed towards my obsessive-compulsive nightmare. "How many are there?" I asked, my head spinning.

"Including the little ones?" Mr. Marshall asked.

"I mean how many do I have to pick from," I said, trying not to hyperventilate.

"Ten thousand," he said matter-of-factly.

I felt weak in the knees. I knew what had to be done—*choose one and choose one fast*. "I see it!" I screamed and ran off towards a Green Giant, while Immy and Jim talked farming with Mr. Marshall.

Immy and Jim found me standing next to a tree just short of Rockefeller Center material. "Scott will kill me," I told them. They looked up at the tree and then at me. *Were they in awe of my choice or figuring out how far it would hang off their truck?* I was trying to keep my eyes on this tree and not let them wander to the hundreds, the thousands of others that were…oh, no, off in the distance I saw a perfectly proportioned beauty, and I walked toward it. As quick as you can say, 'partridge in a pear tree,' I was sucked into the green dimension.

"What time do they close?" I desperately asked as Immy passed me on one of the aisles.

"Well, it gets dark in an hour or so," Immy said. "What size do you want?" I detected in her voice both fear and the realization that I was going to need an intervention.

"Big!" I said, my eyes widening. "Well, sort of big. I mean, it can't be too big. What do you think?"

Immy nodded. "Just walk around a little."

I did. The problem was, I'd pick a tree and try to find someone for a second opinion. On my way to finding someone, I'd see another tree, and I'd suddenly forget where the first one was, or even in which direction. They all looked alike—at least until you got into serious evaluation of their features. At one point I got turned around and stumbled into base camp, where Mr. Marshall was tending to things.

"How do you keep all these trimmed so perfectly?" I asked the handsomely weathered man. "It makes it hard to choose."

"Follow me," he said. "I'll show you."

Why not, I thought, *give my brain some cooling off time*. "When do you start getting ready for Christmas?" I asked the tree farmer as we walked toward his barn.

"August," he said handing me his tool of the trade—The Echo GT 2000 Wonderwand, a weed whacker with jaws. "You know that expression, 'Don't look back?' Well, when I'm trimming I always say to myself, 'Don't look forward.' Because if I look at all the trees I have left to trim, I think I'll die before I finish."

After the tour I headed back into the grove, thinking I might die before I finish or at least be left wandering aimlessly in the dark. Necessity being the mother of invention, I began hanging objects from the trees I liked—my scarf, my hat, a piece of ribbon from my pocket, and a used tissue.

I found Kathy was great at giving a quick, honest evaluation: "Ugly." "Potential, but not this year." "Not good for kids." "Sucks."

I even developed a great tree-hunting vocabulary: *rusty*—the tree equivalent of age spots; *collared*—neckline issues; *a tilter*—needed chiropractic help earlier in life; and *dead*—well, that one explains itself.

As it got darker, I grew frantic and ran to the car to grab my secret weapon. Kathy rounded a pine and caught me in the middle of getting a good angle on a fir. "I know you are not taking Polaroids," she said.

"Yes, I'm taking Polaroids!" I snapped. "You want to get out of here at some point, don't you?"

And with this technique, in the hinterlands of Marshall's, this fool found the perfect tree. I cut it myself. It went something like "Timber!" Flop. "Ouch! Help! I'm stuck under my tree!" After Jim lifted the heavy thing off me, I happily dragged it back to the truck through the darkening dusk.

Scott arrived that night and hailed my find as "the best tree ever." When I told him it only cost thirty dollars, his jaw dropped. "In the city, that would cost at least a hundred!" he bragged, as if he'd bagged the thing himself.

We proudly brought it into the living room, set it in place and began the lighting ceremony. If you've ever strung lights on a Christmas tree, you know the routine. We opened the box of newly purchased lights, pulled each delicate socket out of its plastic noose, and plugged them in. They didn't work. We jiggled them them around. A momentary sparkle was confirmation of a loose bulb.

"You take that end," I instructed. "I'll take this end." We proceeded to check each bulb's hair follicle-sized wire for connection problems, moving along the strand to meet in the middle. I found myself simultaneously wiggling from my end and supervising Scott's end. "I think you just skipped past one," I snapped.

"Did not!" Scott seethed.

"I saw you skip one!"

"I did not."

"Did too!" We continued this back-and-forth until I found the loose bulb.

After that hurdle was jumped, we began stringing the tree. Scott's lack of experience was quickly evident. "You're strangling the thing!" I said. "Watch me! You've got to go in and out along the branches, not just round and round. In and out gives it depth."

"I'm a Jew!" Scott yelled, throwing the strand at me and almost knocking me off the ladder. "Jews don't know Christmas lights. We light Menorahs. Give me a Menorah, and I'll light it."

Fortunately, all fights were forgotten when I finally got the tree lit, and we stood back to admire it.

"Wow," Scott said. "It's beautiful."

"Merry Christmas," I said, holding his hand. "Our first Christmas at Edgewater Farm."

"Let's make it a tradition," Scott said.

"Marshall's with Immy?" I asked.

"No," he said, "that you'll always do the lights."

"Okay," I promised. "It'll be my Christmas gift to our relationship."

22

COUPON CLIPPER

Scott and I were in a mini-mall parking lot stuffing a giant six-foot wide wreath into our five-foot wide trunk. A burly man approached us and asked, "Did you just buy that at Michael's Crafts?"

"Yes," Scott answered proudly while I continued to shove. I had red, white, and blue lights to wrap around this wreath and no time to waste.

"Did you use the coupon?"

"What coupon?" I asked, my left eyebrow rising in a did-I-miss-a-bargain arch.

"Every Sunday, Michael's puts a flier in the paper with a coupon for forty percent off any single item."

"Forty percent off!" Scott choked. "This thing cost eighty dollars. That'd be about…"

"Thirty-five bucks!" I said, yanking the wreath out of the trunk. "I'm taking it back."

"The fliers in the store don't have coupons," the man said. "I already looked. They cut 'em off. So, you'll have to wait until tomorrow."

"For thirty-five bucks, I'll wait." We thanked our fellow Cheap Samaritan and marched back into Michael's.

As we waited in line to return our wreath, I noticed a circular on the counter and got Scott's attention with a quiet *psssst*. "Look!" I said. "There's still a coupon on that one." I quickly snatched the circular so I could use the coupon to return and re-buy the wreath in one easy transaction.

A mousy brown haired, squirrelly woman came to the counter, looked down, and called out, "Hey, Charlene, did you see my circular?" She was standing close enough for me to read her nametag. It said: *Manager*. The flier smoked in my hand like a naughty kid's hot Christmas coal. Scott tried to look innocent.

I gulped. Why I didn't just 'fess up right then, I don't know—maybe it was embarrassment, perhaps it was Christmas stress, or more likely it was because I wanted forty percent off! But what I did next was definitely "Santa's naughty list" material. While one hand called attention to the puff paint kit by the register, the other hand sneakily folded the flier into a distorted origami book and quickly shoved it down the back of my pants.

The disappearance of her flier had Miss Manager truly bewildered. "That's so strange," she told Charlene. "I just spent thirty minutes marking it up with all of next week's specials, and I could have sworn I set it down right there." She tapped the nail of her forefinger on the crime scene counter. "Well, if anybody tries to use the coupon, we'll know. The computer won't let it go through until tomorrow."

A useless hot flier was sizzling in my pants. I felt the sweat drip down my back. I was definitely tattooing myself with flier ink.

"What are you going to do?" Scott whispered.

"Um, I'm going to..."

"Next!" Charlene called. I stepped to the register, along with Scott, my partner in Christmas crime, who was holding our giant eighty-dollar wreath.

"Hi!" I smiled, presenting my receipt and hiding my back. "I just bought this, and I want to return it."

"Return it?" she asked. "What's wrong with it?" Rushing holiday time stood momentarily still.

"Percent coupon. Forty. Tomorrow." I stuttered.

"Oh," Charlene said, studying my five-minute old receipt and my pitiful ashy white face. "I guess in the holiday spirit I could give you the forty percent this one time."

We were both frozen. Finally, Scott sputtered from his shocked stupor: "It won't fit in our car."

I stepped on Scott's foot and said, "He means, we need some rope."

Moments later, we walked out of Michael's with one giant wreath, five yards of cord, and thirty-five bucks richer. I also had a loudly beating tell tale heart.

"I can't believe you just did that!" Scott exclaimed, shaking his head at me as he tied the wreath to the top of the car. "Santa's naughty Christmas karma."

I knew what I had to do. "Okay, I'll meet you in Linens-n-Things." I pulled the creased circular from my pants, ironed it with my palm on top of the hood, and walked back into Michael's. Miss Manager was still looking for Exhibit A, ready to sound the alarms when the Coupon of Tomorrow tried to forty percent its way out the door.

I grabbed a basket, threw in the sweat soaked circular, and picked up a seventy-five percent off pumpkin carving kit. I placed the pumpkin carving kit on top of the circular and non-chalantly made my way over to the unmanned register. I set it down and walked out of the store.

Once outside, I called Michael's and deepened my voice. "Tell the manager her flier is in the basket at the other register," I said. "And have yourself a merry little Christmas."

23

JESUS, MARY, AND JOSEPH

Shortly before buying our house, Scott and I had booked a non-refundable trip for New Year's. Before buying the house, we needed adventure. After buying the house, we needed rest.

We had seriously considered a dogsled expedition in the northern tundra, but would you believe they wouldn't accept dogs? "Is your dog trained to pull a sled," the trip organizer asked.

"Um, no," I admitted. "He wants to ride as a passenger."

"I don't think so," he said, before abruptly hanging up.

We looked into skiing the west, sailing the east, climbing the north, and hiding in the south. We thought of chartering a boat. We thought of London, Sydney, Paris, Hawaii, and Costa Rica... anywhere, as long as they allowed Jasper.

We found our spot off the eastern coast of Puerto Rico on the tiny island of Vieques. It was perfect: an easy flight to San Juan; a small plane to Vieques; a house on the beach; and a Jeep of our own (that Jasper could ride in as a passenger.) Perfect, except for one thing—we discovered that traveling with a pet is nerve-racking. Jasper took his doggie Valium, I took mine, and we boarded the flight to San Juan.

I had everyone—baggage handlers, flight attendants, and even the captain—checking on Jasper. They shut the cabin doors in preparation for take-off, and I got out of my seat and ran to the front of the plane. "My dog has not been loaded on yet," I told the head flight attendant.

A woman on the left side of the plane tapped my arm. "Is that your dog?" she asked. I leaned over her, looked out the window, and saw Jasper riding in his cage up the conveyer belt. He was definitely more relaxed than I was.

When we landed in San Juan, I waited in anticipation for the ground crew to bring Jasper off. "Rest assured, he's fine," the head flight attendant told me proudly. "They do this all the time." As she said this, I watched as Jasper's traveling cage—the Pet Limo—rolled out of the plane, down the luggage loader, and slammed into the large Samsonite ahead of it. Jasper stood up and shook it off. He was headed for baggage claim and so were we. Scott and I had to get Jasper and all our bags from the bowels of the San Juan Airport and to our next gate for a 5:45 departure to Vieques.

At 5:20, when we still didn't have our dog, I strategized. "I'll run ahead and tell them we're here," I told Scott. "You wait for Jasper."

The ticket counter of Vieques Air Link was chaos. A woman was yelling at the counter crew in Spanish. "As I've already told you, it's canceled," the man behind the counter told her. "Bad weather. There's nothing I can do."

I joined the fracas. "Well then, how do we get there?" I asked.

"Unless you're a really good swimmer," he said, "you're not getting there until at least tomorrow."

"What do we do until then?"

"Go have fun in San Juan."

"No, I mean where do we stay?"

"In a hotel," he said.

"We have a dog."

"Oh."

After ten minutes of calls, he found a place that would allow our dog. I must have looked on the verge of meltdown because the man also volunteered to help us get a cab. After a short, yet expensive, cab ride we were dumped outside of Hotel Mario's and stood in silence as we stared at the dislodged "M" and the unlit "r."

"I thought you said Marriott," Scott said accusingly.

"I swear that's what he said. Must be the language barrier."

"It'll do," Scott said as rain began to fall. "It will have to do."

At Hotel Mario's registration counter we were stopped faster than a bad check. "I'm sorreeee," the unangelic receptionist told us in her best Spanish accent. "I chicken out. No dogs allowed." She pointed to a sign behind the counter. "I not want to get fired."

"Can't we just sneak in?" I begged. "You already told us yes."

"I've already seen de dog," she argued. Even my threats of bad karma for her and her entire family didn't work. There was no room at their inn.

We headed into the streets of San Juan pulling our bags, dragging a huge dog cage, and coaxing a travel weary/rain hating canine through a downpour. At least Mary and Joseph had a donkey. As we walked the streets looking for shelter, we noted that Puerto Ricans preferred their dogs in the yard tied to a fence with a short rope not taking luxury vacations.

Finally, at the desk of one motel, a girl who was "just *feeeeling* in" told us the owner would be back "in a few *meeenets*" and might let us have a room. We waited, and waited. A Puerto Rican "*meeenet*" is a lot slower than a New York minute.

When the owner, Ken, arrived, he was on crutches. I told him the story of our struggle and what had happened at Mario's. "You don't want to stay in that roach motel anyway," he said, giving us the keys and the pricey bill for room 105. Joseph and Mary got a stable. We got a street-level, moist-sheeted, sandy-tiled room at Ken's Hotel Casa Blanca. I would have preferred the stable.

Jasper was exhausted from the ordeal and fell asleep on the concave bed. In an attempt to drown out the noise of the registration counter on our shared wall, we turned on the TV and fell asleep to the cuchi-cuchi of Charro on a tacky Spanish variety show.

I won't bore you with the scene at Vieques Air Link the following morning, but I will simply set up the scenario. All of the previous day's passengers, all of that day's passengers, and a dog were vying for a spot on a 9-seat plane and a 14-seat plane. I'm not that good in math, but twenty-three seats will not accommodate fifty travelers and a dog. Fortunately, our eager rush to vacate Ken's had gotten us to the airport really early, and when the 9-seater struggled off the runway, Scott, Jasper and I were on board and on our way to a Happy New Year.

24

ACCIDENT

We returned to New York refreshed. It was a New Year, and we decided to buy ourselves a new car—an all-wheel drive Subaru. I was behind the wheel for our first drive up to the country. The odometer had just flipped to a hundred, and we were on an exit ramp in New Jersey easing toward the merge when, WHAM! We were slammed from behind.

"@$%#! @$%#!" Scott screamed uncharacteristically throwing his cell phone to the floorboard. "Not even a week old and wrecked!"

Yep, I thought. *Happy wreckin' New Year*! I got out of the car and headed to the rear to inspect for damage. Scott angrily stormed out of the passenger side and met me at our bumper in the glare of the perpetrator's headlights. "YOU CAN'T JUST STOP!" Mr. Cream-colored Chrysler Sebring bellowed at me as he got out of his car.

"Excuse me?" I asked, noting that his wife and child were laying low in the backseat, perhaps familiar with both his driving and his anger. "What was I supposed to do? Drive through the car in front of me?" That's when Scott started yelling. Loudly. Bad words. Lots of them spilled onto Route 17 for thirty seconds or so.

While examining his bumper, Mr. Sebring ignored us, and then he turned on his heels and got back in his car. Friday night traffic whizzed by. I ran to get a pen and began to conspicuously write down his license tag.

"What's your problem?" he asked, jumping back out of his car. "What do you think you're doing?" *Not only is he a misogynistic pig*, I thought, *he's stupid.*

"I'm writing down your tag number, Mister," I said, threateningly. "If you leave, it becomes a hit and run."

"Nothing's wrong with your car!" he yelled.

Scott and I turned to look at our Subaru's shiny new bumper in the beams of Mr. Sebring's headlights. He had a point, our car looked fine. "Well, it may have internal bleeding or something," I yelled back. "Or maybe I have whiplash! My neck's hurting."

"He's pulling away! He's pulling away!" Scott chanted.

Yeah, he can run, but he can't hide. I waved my cell phone and the pad of paper on which I'd scrawled his Jersey plate numbers dramatically in the air, and dialed 9-1-1. Mr. Cream-colored Sebring bolted out of his car and stalked towards me. I was sure he was going to punch me.

"Let's pull off the highway," he snarled. "We're in a dangerous spot."

"Okay," I agreed, "but don't try any sneaky business. I've got your tag number."

"...9-1-1, may I help you?"

"Sorry," I said, realizing an emergency operator had been listening to the feud. "Uh, I've been hit. I mean my car's been hit. There's been an accident."

"Is anyone hurt?" the voice asked calmly.

"No," I said, pulling into a parking lot.

"Where are you, sir?" she asked, continuing her routine checklist.

"Route 17 and Route 4."

"Which one, sir? Where exactly?"

I looked up at a flashing yellow sign. "Furniture Liquidators," I said in disbelief. "I'm in the parking lot of a Furniture Liquidators on Route 17 headed north." While we waited for the police, I stared at the array of foam filled sofas and pressed board dressers and pondered the repercussions of my 9-1-1 call.

"Did I do the right thing?" I asked Scott numbly.

"Absolutely," he said. "If you hadn't stopped, you would have hit the car in front of us."

"No," I said. "I mean should I have called the police?" For a moment, I considered driving away. I do, afterall, have an innate fear of police. Flashing blue lights drain the color from my face and I break into a cold sweat. I hit the brakes anytime I see a patrol car, even if I'm in park.

"Well, I guess he could say that you hit him," Scott suggested, contributing to my paranoia.

I became more agitated. "But I'm the one that called 9-1-1," I said. "That should count for something."

"Well," Scott strategized, "just be the first to tell the police what happened."

I glared over at Mr. Sebring sitting behind the wheel, angrily staring forward. His wife and daughter had gone into Furniture Liquidators, hopefully to use the bathroom and not to buy a dining room set. I decided to get out of the car and casually inspect the back of our Subaru, so that when the police arrived it would be obvious that *I* had been hit from behind.

When the Paramus Police pulled into the lot, I immediately jumped into action. "Are you here for me?" I asked the officer. "I'm the one who called '911.'"

"Title, insurance card, and registration," he said stiffly.

I handed him the folder the Subaru dealership had given us, and he quickly perused the documents. "Your registration isn't in here."

We had yet to even open the folder. "We just got the car," I explained. "I know they said they were going to mail us a few things."

"You're supposed to have the registration, sir. You need to find the regi..." I went pasty white. I was having PTSD flashes of rear-ending a brown Pinto shortly after I got my driver's permit. I scurried back over to our car.

"How's it going?" Scott asked.

"Not well. Where's the registration?"

"Everything's in that folder," Scott said confidently.

"Have you even looked in that folder?" I snapped. "No, don't answer that. Just find the registration."

"We're looking for it," I told the officer, my voice trembling. "We just got this car. Our old one gave us a lot of problems and so we spent the Christmas holidays..."

He interrupted me with an attention getting whisper. "Sir, I don't really need to know about your holidays. I just need your vehicle registration."

I returned to the Subaru, snatched the temporary registration off the windshield, and presented it to the Paramus Police. Seemingly satisfied, he wrote down a few numbers. "You can go."

"You mean go back to my car?" I asked. "Or go on my way?"

"Leave," he clarified. "You can leave. If you have any questions or need a copy of the report, you can pick it up after Monday at the Paramus Police Department one block down on Route 17."

"But you haven't heard my side of the story…"

He cut me off faster than a Jersey driver at rush hour. "I don't need to hear your side of the story," he said. "You were hit from behind, and there's no apparent damage. If you need to file an insurance claim, the report will be at the station. Have a nice night."

I stumbled back to the car. "Well, he was handsome," Scott noted.

As I drove up Route 17, I tried to let it go. I wondered what Mr. Sebring told the police and if he was taking out his anger on his wife. Then, I remembered that one of my New Year's resolutions was to look for the good in things. So, I decided that this little drama was sent to me by a Higher Power to either remind me that life cannot be perfect or to give me a story to tell. Either way, I did have to admit that for once Scott was right. "Yep," I said, nodding my head. "That cop was a hunk."

25

SALE SIGNS

A fresh dusting of snow was on the ground in February when, in a move only an addict or an idiot would make, I rolled out of bed and jumped in the car in order to be the first to arrive at the winter's one and only "Moving Sale."

I had seen the sign announcing the momentous event in a fleeting drive by the day before and spent most of the night afterwards dreaming and drooling over the treasures I was sure a Winter Moving Sale would behold. The Moving Outers were definitely going to want to unload their heavy Pyrex and all that old vintage clutter. They certainly wouldn't want to drag that weathered leather club chair to a *new* house! At least this was my working theory as I revved the Subaru's engine at the crack of dawn.

Over the last nine months I'd become an expert hunter, having bagged a lot of finds. In fact, besides the Bloomingdale's living room ensemble, pretty much everything else in the house had been bought on the sale trail. I'd come to know quite a few things about sales in my first ten months of home ownership.

"Garage Sales" typically market household scraps—items that Garagers are too lazy to take to the dump or too greedy to give to the Salvation Army. Instead, they offer for sale such miscellany as three floral saucers without cups, a "Hot Mama" license tag holder, and a collection of chipped and cracked jars. Sometimes, though, amidst the clutter, an "I can't believe they're getting rid of that" moment will occur.

The scene begins with a small gasp escaping accidentally from my lips. During high-hunting season last year, after the gasp I emitted a quick, but audible, squeak. I was casually drifting through the dregs at a garage sale, when, sitting like a jewel on a giant pile of dung, I eyed the matching platter to my set of "Star Glow" dishes. I eased my way to it and flung my arms desperately out like I'd suddenly found my long lost love. I delicately lifted it from a stack of old towels and examined it. No chips, no flakes, no grazing!

I whirled around to ask the all-important question, knocking a bucket of used tennis balls off a makeshift sawhorse table. "How much?" I asked, as tennis balls volleyed about the driveway.

"Hey, Randy!" the Hostess screamed from the comfort of a PVC chaise lounger. "How much you want for your balls?"

"Three dollars!" the squishy former tennis player garbled back through a mouth full of *Snickers*.

"No," I replied, my outsides faking calm, my insides quivering with excitement. "I mean the platter."

"Oh *that?*" the Hostess sneered, wrinkling her nose in disgust. "That's a quarter. There's a matching casserole dish somewhere." I involuntarily clutched my heart. "That's a quarter, too." Moments like that make it all worthwhile.

I chuckled to myself at the memory, turning onto Mill Dam Road with my right hand and picking sleep from my eyes with my left.

"Tag Sales" seem to be one or two *ka-chings* better than Garage Sales… unless a Garage Sale is *posing* as a Tag Sale. Posers can be spotted with a quick drive-by—if an old toilet is displayed out on the lawn atop a paint-splattered drop cloth, buyer be-heavier on the accelerator. At a real Tag Sale one typically finds larger items—like bedroom sets and dining tables—often still in their natural habitat, just with a tag on it.

I once was with a friend who bought an armoire out of someone's bedroom and the clothes inside were included in the sale. One downside about Tag Sale shopping is that the people who run Tag Sales sometimes think they're experts on the Antiques Roadshow.

On occasion, when I don't seem so desperate, Scott accompanies me to sales and sometimes even manages to be interested. At one sale during the heat of last summer, he convinced a woman to try on and then buy a man's red plaid, insulated hunting outfit. "You'll be thanking me this winter," Scott beamed as she modeled the five-dollar ensemble. "It looks hot! And it'll be amazing when it snows." With the thirty inches we've had this year, I'm sure she's thanking him.

My favorite of all sales is the "Barn Sale," but there are only a handful of these preeminent events a year. I discovered the joy of the Barn Sale at the Kern Farm shortly after we first moved in. I got a great many treasures there, including a flip-top desk and an old Victrola with almost a hundred turn-of-the-century records. When someone posts a Barn Sale sign, I'll plan an emergency appendectomy around it.

Today's sale is a "Moving Sale," I reminded myself. *So, don't get your hopes up Littlefield.* Moving Sales are hit or miss. For some reason, some people want to tote the treasures with them when they move and leave the junk behind. But in the winter, I'll take what I can get. *At least*, I promised myself, *today will quench my thirst*, like an alcoholic drinking Thunderbird and liking it.

The first step in any twelve is to admit there's an addiction. So, *"Hello. My name is Bruce, and I'm a junk sale addict."*

When the light rain-snow-ice combo began splattering my windshield, I thought, *Oh good, only the diehards will brave these conditions for an off-season sale.* I veered left off Cottekill Road and onto Sawdust Avenue, passing the sale's droopy cardboard sign narrowly avoiding a woman jogger. "Wacko," I said out loud. I shook my head in disbelief as the steam wafted off her body. *Why would anyone jog in weather like this?*

We came to the end of the road. "Hmmmmph," I grumbled to Jasper, who unlike Scott enjoys my early morning jaunts. "We must have missed it." I turned around and backtracked, slower this time with my eyes peeled. I saw a woman leaning into the trunk of her car and pulled over. As I rolled down the window, she stood up in full curler set and flashed me a *"don't-you-dare-ask-me"* glare. I drove on, keeping lookout for signs of merchandise Mecca.

Wacko, the woman jogger, had also begun backtracking, and I once again swerved to avoid hitting her. My second pass down the road still yielded nothing. Growing evermore frustrated, I stopped and got out to more closely examine the sign, now soggy and smeared. There in crucial teeny tiny letters: "10-4."

"Well," I informed Jasper as I got back in the car, "we have some time to kill." For an hour, we tootled about town getting gas, sipping a cup of coffee and buying some stamps at the post office.

Back on Cottekill Road, Jasper and I sat at the stop sign watching the dashboard's green digital clock tick from 9:54 to 9:57 to 9:59. At 10:00 I launched down Sawdust Road. Still no sign of a sale. At 10:05, I backtracked. Nothing.

Pathetically I drove my car up and down Sawdust Road for twenty-five minutes—at first hoping they were just getting a late start. Then, after coming to terms with the fact that the Moving Sale had probably been *another* Saturday, I looked for a house with a "SOLD" sign in front. I wanted to knock on the door and ask the sellers to step outside so I could explain official sale rules.

I sulked back to the house, and Scott, fresh from an extra two hours sleep, chirped, "How'd it go?"

"Don't ask," I pouted.

"Let me guess," he said, pursing his lips and smartly choking down a chuckle. "Someone left a sign up again?"

Yes, *again*. It's happened several times before and, if it happens again—I'm finding that sorry ass, and I'm going to rifle through his garage until I find the treasures I want. And then, I'm going to demand a discount.

26

SNOWDAY SHOPPING

"Have you heard about the Nor'easter?" Bev asked, when I stopped by the Cat House. It was mid-March and I was desperate to shop.

"The what?" I said, thinking it had something to do with the town egg hunt.

"The big snow storm that's supposed to hit tonight," she explained. Scott and I don't have a television, so our news often comes through the grapevine. "They say we could get up to two feet. You better get your milk and bread."

I sped home to get Scott, and we made a mad dash to the grocery store. Along with what seemed like the rest of the county, we squeezed down the aisles in our down-filled jackets like giant marshmallows.

"Why are we buying milk and bread?" Scott asked as we stood in the Express Lane with our few items. "We don't even drink milk, and I can't think of the last time I ate loaf bread."

But later, when the snowflakes began to fall, I congratulated myself: *At least we're prepared.* I decided the snow was an opportunity to get some serious writing done. Scott decided it was the opportunity for a serious nap. I grabbed the last gulp of orange juice—we forgot to get orange juice!—and headed into the office to turn on my computer.

The only thing more difficult than a driveway of pure white is a screen of pure white, but I felt happily equipped to take on both. I stared as my monitor came to life. *Hmmmmm, let's see...*

I lost myself in thought. Not the thought of my work, but the thought of my house. Harry, the contractor I had considered holding hostage by handcuffing him to the banister, had been working feverishly on the downstairs bathroom and had, at long last, conquered the walls and floors that he described as "*whoop-de-doo'ed.*" (In layman's terms: "big-time crooked.") Given the fact that he had so diligently gotten his work underway, I felt some urgency in finding bathroom fixtures. It was time for some serious shopping.

Shortly after buying the house, I had discovered eBay and now often find myself turning to it to satisfy every spontaneous need, all my middle of the night whims.

The evening I signed up for eBay and named myself "Hellogoodbuys," (clever, huh?) was my most successful bidding night ever. "Look!" I yelled to an uninterested Scott. "Someone's auctioning our dishes. And they're going for cheap." I placed a bid. "More of them!" I announced a few minutes later. I placed another bid. Hellogoodbuys was on a roll.

I repeated this pattern five times and went to bed excited to wake up the next morning and see which of the sets I won. The following morning I had five e-mails announcing five different times: "Congratulations! You were the highest bidder on the Royal-Ironstone Star Glow..."

I gulped and quickly reviewed the eBay rules. Call me blond, but I didn't understand that you're only supposed to bid on *one* of the same type of item at a time and make sure you've lost that one, *before* bidding on another. According to my careful examination of the fine print I had originally ignored, I wasn't required to buy the dishes, but if I didn't I'd get a bad rating and no one would ever want to do business with me again. I made five payments. (And didn't tell Scott.)

The first package arrived. "What's that?" Scott asked.

"I was the successful bidder on some of those Star Glow dishes on-line," I enthused.

"We already have those dishes," he said.

"I thought we should get a few more for entertaining," I finessed.

A couple of days later, three more packages arrived while I wasn't home. I opened the door and was greeted by Scott, who presented me with a package marked "FRAGILE!" and asked, "What is all this?"

"What?" I asked, the color draining from my face. "This box?"

"No, those boxes," he said, pointing to two more packages sitting on the kitchen table. "We have packages from Iowa, Wisconsin, and New Jersey."

"Sssstar Gggglow," I stuttered. "For entertaining."

"For entertaining who? The whole town?"

"Well, we have a lot of friends!"

"But we don't cook!"

"One day we might. I'm planning ahead."

"Send them back," Scott demanded. "Tomorrow."

"Okay." I lied, knowing full well the no refund rule.

The next day the fifth and final package arrived, fortunately while Scott wasn't home. By the time it was all over, we had 37 plates, 19 berry bowls, a dozen soup bowls, coffee service for 20, and a rather large assortment of serving pieces. I displayed as much of the trove our kitchen cabinets could hold and stuck the rest in a box in the basement. But, I promised myself that when I learned how to make a casserole, we'd be inviting the garden club, town council, and high school marching band over for dinner.

Since that infamous first experience with eBay, I've become quite the auctionee. I've developed a winning formula for scoring exactly what I want. It's what I call "the 10 second assault."

After discovering that getting into a messy bidding war days in advance does nothing but drive the price of a desirable item up. Instead, I now wait until the final seconds before an auction ends before placing my extremely way-too-high bid. This gives the unwitting no prior knowledge of my existence and very little reaction time to see that the price on the cherished item has been raised, substantially. I know it's sneaky, but it does require a lot of work and calendar coordination on my part. I've had to leave a dinner party early in order to bid on a vintage "Show-N-Tell" set that Scott wanted, and I rescheduled a meeting in order to nab an antique shuffleboard set. Both I won handily and paid for them by taking out a home equity line of credit.

According to my profile in the "Feedback Forum," the section of eBay in which sellers (thankfully not competing buyers) leave input on how easy or miserable the transaction was, I have noticed that sellers like me. Reeeeeally Sally-Field like me. Some recent comments:

"A Pleasure To Do Business With!! Fast Payment! Good smooth transaction. Good eBayer. Thanks Bruce!"

"Great eBay customer! Prompt, courteous transaction! Highly recommended!"

"Great customer! Prompt emails and lightning fast payment!! RECOMMEND!!! A+++++++++"

Many sellers mention my speedy payment and quick correspondence. That's because when I buy something, I can't wait to get it. With eBay, the adrenaline rush from winning the auction is only the beginning. When I read: "Bidding closed on this item" and see my user I.D. announced as the winner, it's as thrilling as going undetected in a childhood game of "Hide and Seek." I usually yell, "YESSSSSS!" and throw a fist fervently in the air. If I had a football, I would spike it and strut around my living room. Scott, accustomed to my eBay cheers, often groans and asks, "What'd you buy now?"

"WIN!" I remind him. "What did I *win* now..."

The "win" is followed by a friendly congratulatory email from eBay and probable unsportsmanlike jeers from losing bidders. (I've been known to utter a few of those myself.) For a few days after each win, there is a gratification lull until the e-mail arrives from the seller announcing that the item has been shipped.

Delivery day is as fun as Christmas morning, except for the mess caused by all the crunchy packing noodles.

Sometimes, I am so consumed by not writing, but by winning an item such as an "Antique Toilet Paper Holder" for our bathroom, that I lose track of everything else going on, like near blizzard conditions whirling around outside. It wasn't until after I had my toilet holder triumph that I realized the snow outside had caused a slight problem. We were snowed in. At least two feet of snow had piled against the screen door in as many hours.

I looked down at Jasper whose time to go had come. "Sorry, boy," I said. "I can't open the door. You're going to have to hold it for a little while."

When Immy called to say Jim was running behind on the plowing because of road closures, I took matters into my own hands. I put on my boots, climbed out the kitchen window, and carefully tromped through knee-deep snow to my front door.

In retrospect, the Sasquatch-type footprints I so carefully embossed from the driveway to my front door didn't work out as well as I had envisioned. I thought convenient indentations in the snow would make the walk secure and slip-free, but later, when it turned to ice, some guests found it difficult to match my stride in the sculpted frozen foot formations. In the future, I decided I'd take the extra time and shovel the walk. The eBay deliveries have to get to the front door!

27

EASTER FASHIONS

I awoke on Easter morning to a basket filled with goodies. While I munched on a chocolate bunny, Jasper drooled on my leg. "Mine," I said authoritatively. "Chocolate bunny bad for Jasper." He understands abbreviated sentences, and food is his favorite conversation.

The lingering chill in the air left the blooms feeling less than inspired, but as Scott, Jasper and I drove down the road I caught a few fleeting glimpses of forsythia yellow and crocus purple. Churches were spilling synthetic color onto their lawns—and into the road.

"Watch out!" I shrieked. Scott ground the recently repaired Wagoneer (now part of our growing fleet of vehicles) to a halt. An errant egg hunter in brightly dyed taffeta had hopped onto the road. The taffeta'd toddler was quickly followed by a woman wearing what looked like bright pink drapes. Her outfit was as horrible as her scream.

"Sorry," she mouthed to us as she toted her toddler back onto the lawn.

I waved to the twosome and pouted to Scott, "I didn't get a cute Easter outfit this year."

"You didn't need one," he said. "We're not going to church, we're going to move a sofa."

Oh yeah. Scott and I had agreed to help Immy and Jim move a sofa. In their "'tis better to give than receive" way of life, they had discovered a sofa for our friend Lee that their daughter Kathy was giving away. We'd just have to go pick it up. *Easy*. Yeah, right.

The Serta Perfect Sleeper eagerly unfolded as we—as Scott and Jim—carried it to the truck. Immy and I followed along behind, picking up errant pillows and trying to keep the movers in line. When we finally got the couch nested neatly on the back of their truck, Immy suggested that we go get lunch.

As you may suspect, Easter at an establishment named *The Rainbow Diner* was quite colorful. While I munched, I also gawked at the gravity-defying hairdo of a woman at the counter. "Now that's Aqua Net in action," I noted. "Grandma Pearl would be proud, huh Scott?"

"She'd have to buy an extra roll of Charmin to wrap it up," he laughed. Scott's 80-something-year-old Grandma Pearl had wrapped her "do" in toilet paper every night of her adult life. According to Pearly, it "keep*sh* it ni*she* and neat*sh*."

The only time I've ever seen Pearly upset was when Scott and I went to visit her in Florida and took her for a ride in a rented

Mustang convertible. "I hate to be a kill-joy!" she screamed from the backseat as we whizzed through Palm Beach. "But if we don't put the top up, I'm going to be *sh*ick."

"You're not going to be sick," I laughed, watching in the rearview mirror as she held her hairdo down. Well, in place. "Enjoy it, Pearly. When have you ever ridden in a convertible?"

"Never!" she hollered through the breeze. "And thi*sh* i*sh* why!" She let go of her hair for only a second, but in that brief moment her hair took the form of a giant swirl of soft serve ice cream. One big auburn twisted follicle.

I immediately pulled over and put the top up. Until the day she died, Grandma Pearl told the harrowing tale of "what the convertible did to her hair" as if she had survived a plane crash. Scott and I once tried to figure out how many rolls of toilet paper Pearl had gone through in her lifetime. We calculated: four rolls a week, 52 weeks a year, 50 years of rolling—Grandma Pearl had unrolled enough to mummify at least 700 Mr. Whipples.

"This diner waitress and Grandma Pearl," I said, "should meet and compare notes."

After lunch, a more full foursome and Jasper (happy with his two fries) headed to deliver the sofa to our friend Lee. Immy and Jim were ahead in their truck; Scott and I were following in the Wagoneer. At this point, you're probably guessing that something went horribly awry. Did the couch slide off the truck? Nope. Did Scott and Jim crash? No. Did we get pulled over for too wide a load? Nah. The couch delivery actually went off without a glitch—save for one minor trouble. Lee's front door had to be removed to get it through, which did take a few extra minutes and tools.

After the successful move, we all stood on the porch, enjoying the early spring air. "Where's Jasper?" I asked.

"Oh, he's exploring," Lee said.

"Believe me," I said assuredly, "if he's not here, he's off finding something to eat." After a few minutes of calling, I got him to come with a sneaky: "Hey Jasper, you want a treat?" He sauntered onto the porch, looking as guilty as a kid who'd been caught with his hand in the cookie jar.

"Where ya been, boy?" Scott asked. After a brief inspection turned up no evidence of wrongdoing, we decided it was time to go. We had one more thing to pick up at Kathy's: a bookshelf for Jim and Immy. We waved our goodbyes, and Jasper lethargically climbed into my lap on the front seat. Halfway to Kathy's, Jasper's stomach kicked like a donkey and before I could get the words out of my mouth, the entire contents of Jasper's stomach came out of his into my lap, oozed down my legs, and seeped into my shoes.

"*Aaaaaaah*!" I convulsed. "*Aaaaaaaah*!" I was coated in what looked like black coffee grinds and what smelled like poop.

Scott burst into grossed out laughter. "It's not funny!" I cried. "I'm going to throw up. You know I have a weak stomach." My entire family does. My mother often recounts the nauseating story of one Disney vacation in which we drove home in a van full of vomit. My sister's yuke had caused my brother to yuke and that had caused me to yuke. It is a rubber laying, emergency lane rattling memory I'll never forget.

"What should I do?" Scott asked, trying to choke back laughter as I tried to choke down vomit.

"Just drive," I barked.

"Are you okay, Jasper?" Scott cooed sympathetically. "What'd you eat, boy?"

"Whatever it was, it's all out on me," I belched. "Drive faster."

"Emergency!" Scott announced with lights flashing and horn honking as we pulled into Kathy's driveway. "Bruce is covered in throw up."

I stepped out of the car dripping black poop smelling granules.

"Ewww," Immy said, scrunching up her nose. "That's Malorganite."

"What's that?"

"You don't want to know."

"Yes, I do."

"No, you don't," she insisted. "It's an organic fertilizer made out of processed human feces."

"Shit!" I took off my clothes as I ran down the sidewalk towards Kathy's. "Find me something to wear, Immy!" Kathy had emptied the house of all her clothes in preparation for her summer renter. As I showered off, I heard Immy scurrying around the house opening doors and slamming drawers, so I knew the outfit was going to be less than perfect.

"Have you found anything, Immy?" I yelled through the crack of the bathroom door.

"Well," she said, "this is all I could find." Her arm came into the bathroom.

"You've got to be kidding." She wasn't. It was literally the only garment in the house. It was that or my vomit-covered outfit. I chose *that*.

I walked out of the house. "Golly!" Jim chuckled. "Nice legs."

"Shut up," I said, angrily sashaying to the car. "Let's go. We can all laugh about this later."

Jim and Immy took off ahead of us with the bookcase, and we pulled out after them. When we turned onto Lucas Avenue, I heard heaving in the backseat. "Pull over!" I told Scott. "He's going to throw up. Pull over right now!" Scott screeched the Wagoneer to a halt on the side of the road, and I jumped out of the car and opened Jasper's door.

I stood over Jasper, soothingly talking to him as if he were one of my drunk and puking dorm mates in college. A car passed, honking and catcalling. "What are you looking at?" I screamed back at them. "Haven't you ever seen a dog barf?!" Suddenly, in one horrifying moment I realized what they were looking at was *me* in my Easter outfit—a pink satin Victoria's Secret negligee, hitting my thighs like a Tina Turner mini-skirt.

Sometimes you get what you ask for.

28

RAISING THE ROOF

The Nor'easter proved our home inspection prognosis wrong—our roof didn't have the "two to five years left in it" that the report had suggested, it had less than one. We had a waterfall in our guest bedroom that wasn't part of a Frank Lloyd Wright designed architectural element.

The first estimate for replacing our roof came in at over seventeen thousand dollars. I couldn't believe it when the man gave me the quote. In fact, I said exactly that: "I can't believe it!"

"I just did De Niro's," he bragged. "*Youse* heard of him, right? I'm the best. Trust me, *youse* get what *youse* pay for."

Perhaps. But Scott and I thought a few more estimates were in order. One guy came over and, after walking on our roof for about an hour, climbed down the ladder and told me, "Yeah. I can do it. It'd run you about eight thousand dollars."

"Great!" Eight thousand dollars was still an incredible amount of money, but after De Niro's guy, it sounded like a bargain. "When can you start?"

"October."

"It's April," I reminded him, thinking he was calendar-dyslexic.

"I've got a long waiting list."

The next guy was movie star good-looking, a young Marlon Brando. When I opened the door and saw him standing on the front porch with his ladder, my first thought was he'd be worth a little extra. "Do you mind looking at my back," he said, lifting his shirt. "I think something just bit me." As I inspected his muscles, I came to the conclusion that hiring him might cost me too much stress.

We ended up hiring a man with three-and-a-half fingers. He brought samples like a Fuller brush salesman and proudly displayed them on the tailgate of his truck. After much deliberation, we picked a speckled gray architectural shingle, layered like a cedar shake roof. "I've been in the business 35 years," he claimed. "And my son and I do all the work ourselves." He handed us a long list of references (with addresses and phone numbers) and quoted us a price of twelve thousand dollars.

Scott and I exchanged The Look and I said, "Let's do it." Little did I know when I wrote the man a deposit check for six thousand dollars and shook his three-and-a-half fingered hand that I would eventually shoot him the middle of my five.

Three-and-a-Half Fingers called me in the city a few days into the project to explain that he was going to have to adjust his estimate. Upward. As it turned out, he "hadn't been aware" when he made the estimate that our roof had more layers on it than an Eskimo in winter. The extra layers were going to require his men extra work and that was going to cost us, well, "a little extra."

"How much?" I asked.

"A thousand."

"A thousand dollars!" I squealed. I should have known right then to stop the project and put an end to the madness. We could camp in our tent when it rained. But instead, desperate to get the work done (and needing, I suppose, a good screw) I said, "Okay, but no more surprises. Agreed?"

The next day, I arrived home to a message on our machine from 3½. This time to say that they couldn't get a thirty-yard dumpster down the driveway, and it was going to cost "a coupla hundred dollars extra" for two twenty-yard dumpsters.

"That's it," I said to Scott over dinner in the city. "I'm heading up there tomorrow morning."

I arrived the next day before 3½ and his son. It had rained the night before. In fact, it had poured, forcing me to dodge puddles the size of Lake Erie as I pulled my car down the driveway. What I saw at the house left me in complete horror. There sat our farmhouse as bald as a baby's butt. Blue tarps were dangling off of it and flapping in the breeze.

The ceilings upstairs were spongy wet and dripping fat raindrops all over the floor of my house. I was ready to pounce on 3½ and bite off at least a finger more with my teeth. I waited and waited for his arrival. Nothing. By noon with no return call to my continued beeps and messages, I decided that they were never coming, so I journeyed out to get some errands done and try to cool down.

When I returned late that afternoon, there were two trucks parked in the driveway and five men I'd never seen were working on my roof. Neither his truck or 3½ was on the property, but the five unknowns had started laying shingles over the wet roof. What I could easily see with my naked, untrained eyes was that the shingles weren't level. In fact, they were crooked, pitched like a ski slope.

"Excuse me," I hollered up as they hammered. No response. "Excuse me!"

"Huh?" one of them finally called down.

"Who are you?" I asked.

"We're the roofers, the owner's not home."

"I am the owner! Get off my roof." They looked at me like I had 3½ eyes. "Right now!" None of these men were the man I'd hired to do the job and none of them was his son either. As I discovered, they were "subcontractors," basically, unemployed workmen that 3½ had hired and put to work.

I asked the fattest one, the guy who seemed like the leader, to follow me. I walked to the back of the garden, turned around, and pointed back at the house. "Do you notice anything unusual about the shingles?" I asked him.

"Well, they aren't finished."

"No. Try again."

"They're speckled?"

"No. Look closely at the roof line."

"Uh huh," he grunted.

"Now, look at the shingles."

"Okay."

"Can you not see that they're crooked?" I asked.

"I think that's just what they call a mirage," he said, seriously. "It's just 'cause it ain't finished. You'll see when it's finished, it'll look straight."

"Sir, with all due respect, I know straight and that's not it. I want you to get in your truck and get out of my yard. And please tell the man who hired you that I'M REALLY PISSED!"

The following afternoon 3½ showed up at the house. Scott had come to the country to help me deal with the situation, or more likely, to prevent a homicide. We all stood in the yard, staring at the bald house with the crooked transplant line. "Yep," he agreed. "It's crooked."

Fingers went on to spill his sob story, saying that he had taken on too much work and admitted, under my machine gun cross-examination, that yes, he had lied by saying that he and his son would do the work. "I'll make it good," he swore. "I'll make it right. You have my word as a gentleman." Then, he offered me his 3½ finger handshake and spoke the words that still reverberate in my head: "I want to be your friend."

The next day, he and his son plucked the crooked rows of shingles out of the roof and started again. By afternoon, there was a sufficient enough amount of work done that I felt it was safe to return to the city. That was my mistake.

When I returned on the weekend, our roof was indeed finished, and it was level, but the gardens around the house were obliterated; the Japanese maple mangled; there were cigarette butts sprinkled throughout the yard; two lightning rods were missing; and someone had walked not on the beams of our roof but on the ceiling of the upstairs beneath them. When I laid my head on my bed that night, the bedroom ceiling had more cracks than a plumber's convention.

When 3½ came by for his check, I couldn't say a word. All I could do was stand on the porch shooting him the bird, while Scott politely told him that it would be a cold day in hell before he ever saw another dime from us.

That night as we soaked in the Jacuzzi I tried to find the rainbow amidst the clouds. "Let's look at it this way," I told Scott. "We only spent six thousand dollars on a twelve thousand dollar roof."

"Yeah," Scott agreed, finding his own bright side. "I guess we don't have to fix the cracked ceilings right away."

The next weekend Scott greeted a couple at our front door. "A referral?" I heard him say. "Are you serious?" 3½ had added our name to his long list of referrals. "Let me show you around," Scott said, his face unusually serious. I watched as he and the twosome walked around our yard, Scott animatedly pointing out the atrocities as he talked. The tour concluded upstairs with an examination of cracks in our bedroom. As he said goodbye to our guests, Scott said nicely, "Do me a favor. Tell him he might want to take us off his list of references."

29

BARN SALE

When Immy told me that she was going to have a Barn Sale, I knew it was going to be BIG. She'd been collecting stuff in that barn of hers for ten years. "Do you think having it on the Saturday of Memorial Day weekend would be okay?" she asked as we planted my cottage's new shade garden.

"You need to start your sale on Friday morning," I advised. "That way you'll get the dealers."

"I really don't think people will come," Immy doubted, her hands covered in compost. "Nobody will want our junk."

"First of all, it's not junk, Immy," I instructed. "It's 'treasure.' Second of all, you're obviously going to need help pricing." I volunteered. *That way*, I schemed, *I'll be the first in line.*

For several weeks, the Barn Sale was postponed due to buckets of rainy weather. During this time, like Joseph, I had a dream.

"Immy," I croaked into the phone upon waking from my big, big dream. "You're going to make enough money from your sale to buy the hot tub you've always wanted for your porch."

"*Noooooooo*," Immy gasped. "I'm telling you, we really don't have that much valuable stuff."

Her sale proved that Immy was wrong—she did have that much valuable stuff—and my dream was right, sort of. She and Jim could have soaked on their porch in a joyfully relaxing pool of effervescent bubbles had a furry detour not soaked them first.

"Signage is the key to a great sale," I coached Thursday afternoon before Friday's grand opening. I ticked off the perfect sign attributes: big, dark letters; arrows pointing in the right direction; dates, times, and address. "Put them up, and they will come."

5:45 a.m. Friday morning, clear skies. My alarm clock buzzed, announcing that the Sale of the Century had finally arrived. I wearily rolled over and told Jasper that he could stay in bed. He lifted a heavy lid, revealing one bloodshot eye, and fell promptly back to sleep. I quickly threw on clothes and staggered out to the car.

6:25 a.m. Davenport's Fruit Stand. "Heading to the city?" Betty asked, as I shuffled past the pallets of plants that, given the early hour, hadn't been put out yet.

"Nope, Betty," I yawned. "Barn Sale. Immy's having a Barn Sale."

6:50 a.m. County Route 6. I passed Jim in his truck zooming around a curve, obviously on a sign-hanging mission. I honked and waved.

6:55 a.m. I saw a perfectly painted sign heralding Immy and Jim's address, along with sale dates and "9 a.m. to 6 p.m.," posted at the start of their road. I rumbled down the driveway and saw Immy standing by the barn. I could tell immediately that she was not a happy woman.

"I am so mad at Jim I can't stand it," she seethed. "I know he threw the bag with my price tags in it into the fire." Immy had gotten garage sale price tag stickers. She'd proudly shown them to me the day before during our sign-planning discussion—round, neon-colored stickers printed with varying amounts from 10¢ to $20.

"I'm sure they're here somewhere," I said, trying to keep the day positive.

"He throws everything into that damn fire," Immy grumbled, dumping a box of pulleys onto a table. "How much do you think for these?"

"Ten bucks. Sell 'em as a set," I decided. "We should hurry, Immy, people will be here soon."

"We have two hours," Immy said as she fretted about looking for her damn neon-colored stickers. "The signs say '9 a.m.'" I stopped my frenetic pricing pace to explain to Immy that once the signs were up her sale was fair game. As I finished my explanation, a blue mini-van with "I BUY POSTCARDS" painted on the side zoomed down the driveway.

7:20 a.m. Before we could say "a quarter," the Barn Sale had begun.

By 8:00 a.m. Immy had found the price tags (she'd left them behind the barn), Jim had forgiven Immy's incendiary "pyromaniac" accusations, and *Immy and Jim's 9 a.m. Barn Sale* had a crowd. I had also spent $273.

8:55 a.m. Out of money and late for a conference call, I rolled down the window of the Subaru to give Immy my parting words of advice: "Now, if someone asks if you can do better today, say, 'It's the first day of the sale. Why don't you check back on Sunday? Everything left will be half price.' Either they'll pay full price, or they'll be back." She leaned in the car, kissed me, and I backed up the driveway past a flock of incoming bargain hunters.

Throughout the rest of the day, my hourly calls to Immy's cell phone were greeted with "Can't talk, got a crowd," or "Lots of people here, I'll call you back," or "That'll be forty-two dollars." I knew it was going well.

6:20 p.m. Jim knocked on my front door to say he had the old doctor's examination table and glass cabinet I had bought in the back of his truck. We unloaded the treasures, and Jim unpacked a piece of interesting news. "Immy couldn't come," he explained. "She's waiting on the Puppy Lady."

"The Puppy Lady?" I asked.

"She's bringing a couple of deer chasing dogs for us to look at," Jim revealed with a thud. Jim's truck hadn't even pulled out of the driveway before I had Immy on the phone.

"Deer chasing dogs?" I quizzed.

"A Great Pyrenees," Immy enlightened me. "He is *sooooo* cute."

"You didn't…"

"I did." With a portion of her first day's windfall, Immy bought a dog.

"A puppy wasn't in my dream, Immy," I yelped.

"We're paying half in cash," Immy explained, "and the Puppy Lady is going to take the other half from whatever merchandise we have left on Sunday."

Puppy Lady, as Immy was to learn from several of the Barn Sale attendees over the weekend, was notorious in these parts. A neighboring town is even taking her to court. One man who had bought two husky mixes explained, "She sucks you in, and you have no breath left when she's done with you." He's still waiting for repayment on the "money back guarantee" after returning the "very calm" dogs that had torn his house to shreds.

Saturday. Scott and I made our way over to the Barn Sale to meet the Deer Chaser. We found the little white furball asleep beneath Immy's clematis arbor, but sure enough no deer were in sight. Perhaps that was due to the all-out party atmosphere that had become *Immy and Jim's Barn Sale.*

Neighbors Mack and Yvonne had picked up a few of the more offbeat items—a Model T car horn, a tamborine, and a cane—and were using them to entertain the crowd with a vaudevillian style act. Mack, self-appointed ringmaster, donned a baseball cap with deer antlers and was acting like a side show barker. "Come take a free tour of an incredible built-from-the-land log home," he heralded. "It'll just cost you five bucks to get back out!"

By the time we left, Scott had bought a Levi's t-shirt with "HARD" written across the front in big letters, and I had purchased a blue and white oil painting entitled "*the end was seen by the kool-aid queen.*"

Sunday. Immy and Jim's sale became an all out Barn Storming party, a "Take what you want giveaway."

Immy gave me the end of sale report. "You know that dresser?" she asked. "That went for five dollars."

"Five dollars!" I screamed. "That was priced at fifty dollars."

"Yeah," Immy chuckled, "But we discovered it had been mothballed and varnished over. It sort of stunk." Apparently, the girl who bought it was thrilled, especially when Jim offered to deliver it. That one had even shocked Immy. "You're going to deliver a five dollar dresser to Stone Ridge?" she asked her husband of forty years.

"Five dollars!" he said, dropping his jaw. "The last time I looked that dresser was fifty dollars."

"Everything's on sale today," Immy reminded him.

Immy's favorite gang was a bunch of kids with blue and pink hair. Every pierceable part of their bodies—and even some of the not so pierceable—was ringed, cuffed, and bejeweled.

"Rudy?" one girl asked her friend. "Give me another quarter. These books are six for a dollar, and I want to get six."

"Honey," Immy grinned in a state of Barn Sale bliss, "For you, they are six for seventy-five cents."

"Reeeeeeeally?" the girl squealed euphorically, throwing her arms around Immy. "You are sooooo nice."

Before the kids with the multi-colored hair left, Immy grabbed a pink hat and plopped it on top of a cute girl's head. "Here," Immy said, smiling triumphantly. "You have to have this. It matches your hair."

So, lots of people got lots of treasures and had lots of fun. And Immy and Jim are a puppy away from my dream of a back porch hot tub.

30

DRIVING ME CRAZY

Scott can't drive. Although he'll tell you differently, this is a fact that has been anxiously confirmed by anyone who has ever ridden with him. "I drive *fine*," he insists, while swerving into oncoming traffic as he adjusts the air conditioning. "You're just a nervous Nellie."

"Only when I'm in the car with you," I sneer.

Another known fact—each and every time he drives, we have a fight. One recent trip started with a difference of opinion before we'd even gotten in the car. Scott decided he wanted to take a flower arrangement from the city to the country for the long weekend so that, as he put it, we could "continue to enjoy them." After he spent about ten minutes looking for the appropriate traveling vessel, I grabbed the flowers out of his hand, wrapped the stems in soggy paper towels, and stuck them into a plastic grocery bag.

"Done," I announced. "Let's go."

Out at the car, wedged between the bumper of our Outback and the grill of an Isuzu Trooper, was when things really heated up. Eager to get to the country, I was shoving our bags into the car with one arm and pulling Jasper with the other. All Scott had to deal with was the bouquet, which he went to put in the back of the car. "Watch out!" I instructed. "Those lilies are loaded with pollen."

"Can't you just let me do something without suggesting a better way?" he barked, carelessly tossing the flowers into the back and sprinkling orange powder across the upholstery.

"Sure I can," I spat. "But then you go and do something genius like that."

"No big deal," he said, using his hand to rub the pollen off. Or, more precisely, rub the pollen in. I mumbled angrily beneath my breath. "What'd you say?" he asked.

"Nothing you'd want to hear," I huffed.

"It sounded like you called me 'stupid.'"

"Did it?" I provoked. "Well, it certainly was stupid, but I'm not sure that's what I said." Our squabble was interrupted by our superintendent who walked out of our building and unsuspectingly into the line of fire. We momentarily called a truce and made small talk with him about our weekend plans, but the moment he walked away, we picked up where we left off.

"Get in the car," Scott seethed.

"Fine." As anyone in a serious relationship will tell you, "fine" means—"Not fine. Not over."

Scott peeled onto West End Avenue, jostling all the car's contents and occupants dramatically to the left. "Watch out!" I yelled. "You almost ran over that little old lady."

"I was a mile away from that little old lady."

I looked back. "Oh yeah? I suppose she's shaking her fist in the air because she's finally conquered the need for Depends."

"Just shut up," he instructed.

"Fine."

Scott is always the first to forget we're fighting. He's also the first to forget he's driving. Not a mile across the George Washington Bridge, I caught him with his neck craned backwards. "Is that a brushfire?" he asked, his head facing where we'd been, rather than where we were going.

The car headed toward the median. "Scott!" I screamed, holding my knotted stomach. "You're swerving all over the road. You can't look back when you're driving forward."

"I didn't swerve," he insisted. "It was just a hiccup."

"That wasn't a hiccup," I countered. "That was a convulsion."

Scott then suggested that instead of arguing the entire drive up the New York State Thruway, we should listen to our *Berlitz Italian Audio Guide*. We had planned a trip to Tuscany and decided to brush up on our Italian. Well, Scott was brushing up; I was doing more of a comb-over.

I'm no linguist. In my childhood, there was only one language—Southern—and my family spoke it perfectly. Foreign language acquisition is not one of the Littlefields' greatest skills. In fact, during my family's one European vacation, my Dad humiliated us by showing off his south German. We—my brother, sister, Mom, Dad, and enough luggage to start an American Tourister outlet—crammed into a tiny Yugo. The Yugo was Dad's idea of "saving money where we can." With our knees tucked to our chins, the backseat looked like a school hallway in a 1950s "How To Survive a Tornado" film. But, hey, we were saving ten dollars a day.

For a week, we putted down the Autobahn. We journeyed from Germany through Austria and Czechoslovakia. On our last day, we were detained by armed guards at the border of Hungary, where, after unloading us and all our luggage like clowns in a circus, it was finally decided that no spies, drug dealers, or terrorists would be dumb enough to fold themselves into a Yugo. Getting everything back into the Yugo was a feat of engineering, and due to the Hungarian incident, we returned to Germany late for our flight.

We could tell that we were close to the airport by the Yugo-rattling fly-overs of jumbo jets, but we couldn't seem to find the route in. Every road seemed to lead us back to the same intersection where a group of construction workers were doing road repairs. Finally, realizing that there was no other way, my Dad succumbed and stopped to ask the construction team for directions. "Hey!" he hollered out the window. "Could ya'll tell me how to get to the airport?"

They responded with something that sounded to us like: "*spickenzy dein awf ick ick dein spickenzy.*"

"Air-port?" my Dad asked again, this time slowly, adding sign language by flapping his hands like wings. The construction team leaned on their shovels and shrugged their shoulders. Then, in a dramatic effort that will always live in infamy in my family, my Dad decided to attempt German, and in his South German drawl asked, "*Whicha way-a to the air-ee-uh-porta?*"

The workers laughed hard. We knew they were laughing because laughter in German sounds exactly like it does in English—especially when you're the family in a Yugo being laughed at. From my tucked position in the backseat, I pointed to a passing plane like Tattoo on Fantasy Island and said, "The plane, the plane." The construction workers looked up in the sky, nodded as if they got it, and then pointed down the road.

Dad hit the gas on the Yugo, and we lurched forward. After going in a circle twice—both times forced to pass the pointing and hooting construction workers—we made it to the airport. As I separated from my parents for my solo flight back to New York, I swore three things: 1) I'd never get into another Yugo; 2) I'd never travel to Europe again with my Dad; and 3) The next time I went to a foreign country, I'd learn a little of the language.

So it was that Scott and I bought the Berlitz CD and, in our attempt to get over the driving fight, began learning "practical Italian."

"Are you ready to learn Italian?" the woman's voice cooed over music that conjured images of bad 1970s porn.

"Yes!" I agreed.

"*Si*," a man's voice on the CD answered.

"Oh, yeah," I said, catching on, "*si*." I had learned my first Italian word! I was confident and ready for more.

"We'll begin with basic expressions," the woman continued. "Follow along in your guidebook if you like."

"Yes," the woman's voice cued.

"*Si*," Scott and the man's voice harmonized.

"*Si*," I echoed a moment later.

"No," the woman's voice cued.

"*Non*," Scott and the man's voice dueted.

Scott's driving distracted me. "You better slow down," I told him.

"Just listen to the lesson," he ordered. The distraction got me lost, and from the next page on, I was the slow learner in need of remedial classes. While Scott learned "okay," "thank you very much," "hi," and "good morning." I desperately tried to catch up.

"Do you speak English?" the woman asked.

"*Parla inglese?*" the man's voice echoed. Knowing that one would be vital to my Italian success, I hit repeat on the CD player at least a dozen times to catch it. I also wore out the repeat button on, "Does anyone here speak English?" which is "*C'e qualcuno qui che parla inglese?*" and "I don't speak much Italian," which is "*Non parlo italiano molto bene.*"

As we neared our exit on the Thruway, flashing lights whirled behind us. I watched in the rearview mirror as Scott tried to talk the cop out of a ticket, simultaneously mastering the one phrase I wouldn't leave home without: "*Non capisco,*" which is Italian for "I don't understand."

When Scott got back in the car with a ticket in hand, his face was whiter than my untanned behind. He was gurgling on and on about being "sure" he wasn't going "83."

All I could say was, "*Si, si, si.*"

For Scott's trial a few weeks later, I cleverly concocted a fail-safe plan to get him out of the ticket, involving "lots of cars around us at the time," and cruise control and, the biggest laugh of all, "I'm the most cautious driver."

After the trial, Scott called me proudly to proclaim: "Only two points."

"Two points?!" I cried, envisioning the new insurance bill. "Did the judge not buy your story?"

"I decided not to go to trial," he explained. "They told me instead of six points, I could pay the fine and settle out of court for two."

"*Non capisco* you" was all I could think of to say.

31

TRYING TO COOK

On our way up to the country, Scott broke some exciting news. "I'm going to start taking violin lessons," he said. I nearly swerved into the big giraffe on the side of a Toys-R-Us eighteen-wheeler.

"What do you mean?" I asked, my insides shaking and my eye suddenly twitching. With sincerest apologies to all current and future Itzhak Perlmans, I *hate* the nerve-rattling squeal of a violin. And one thing I know about Scott is that when he takes something up, he goes at it whole hog.

His hobbies have long been life changing. I spent hours at the bookstore when Scott practiced the tin whistle. I bought noise-cancelling headphones when he studied the mandolin. I was an accessory to the quiet crime of photography, buying several expensive camera-related presents for that one. He never broke his leg ice-skating, though he did dislocate his knee. And, except for the odor of incense, Buddhism was relatively harmless, thank God.

I will say that I enjoyed his artistic period. He's actually from a family of artists (his grandfather Mo Leff was the hand behind the Joe Palooka cartoons, and his grandfather Edward Stewart was the Academy Award winning set decorator for *All That Jazz.*) After I framed several of Scott's paintings and hung them on the wall, he decided that he didn't like being an artist. So, he packed up his paints and moved on. Most recently, I bought him a reflective vest for his triathlon training. The jury is still out on that one.

But violin lessons? No. "I'm sorry, Scott. I cannot, will not, shall not tolerate the sound of a violin in the house. Ever!" I couldn't have been any clearer. "Why don't you take up something that we can both enjoy together?" I asked.

"Like what?"

"How about cooking lessons?" We had fallen off our "we'll make dinner three nights a week" promise. We weren't even capable of doing two. Cantaloupe and cottage cheese got very boring, even when topped with strawberries. But I am proud to say we have perfected a new meal: couscous topped with grilled shrimp/vegetable kabobs served with homemade Caesar salad. *Everything* is homemade. Okay, the couscous is out of the box, but I don't think it comes any other way. And the Caesar salad is out of the bag for the same reason. But otherwise, it's all homemade.

"Okay," Scott agreed. "I'll make dinner this weekend." With city friends coming to visit us in the country, I was a little hesitant to start our cooking hobby so ambitiously and campaigned for Ming Moon Chinese takeout. "Trust me," Scott said. "We can serve dinner for six. We'll do our shrimp kabobs and couscous."

"Okay," I agreed. "Safety in the already tested."

It was on the couscous aisle that our plan went awry. "What do you mean there's no couscous?" Scott asked after I found him at the seafood counter. "They can't be out of couscous."

"There is an empty spot on the shelf where the couscous box should be," I explained. "It goes from basmati rice to risotto."

"Hmmm. What do you think we should do instead?" Scott quizzed.

"Let's order from Ming Moon," I suggested. "We can just put it in our bowls." That's when I caught sight of the catch in his hands. He was holding two packs of tuna. "What are you doing with that tuna? Where's the shrimp?"

Then, he uttered the words that would change our night (and perhaps our guests' stomachs) forever: "I thought we could try something *different*." The word "different" bounced around the store like a bad boob job. "Tuna kabobs."

"But they don't have any couscous," I begged. "Please, let's just get Chinese takeout."

Dinner for six. Seven o'clock.

Back at home, while Scott began slicing and dicing a rainbow assortment of peppers, I made cocktails, somehow knowing that we'd need them. I had insisted that we buy a pack of shrimp to mix on the kabobs and pencil asparagus as a side. "Plain tuna seems awfully boring," I had pleaded.

When our first guest arrived, I immediately shoved a cocktail in his hand. "Consider it an appetizer," I joked.

When our other friends arrived, Scott lit the stove to start the basmati rice. I stopped him. "Why don't you get everything prepped and ready to cook?" I whispered. "And let's go into the living room and talk to our guests for a while." Whether he thought that was a good idea or not, he complied. After the second round of cocktails, Scott started the rice and fired up the grill.

He came back into the kitchen while I was tossing the Caesar salad. "You can start the asparagus," he suggested, holding some kind of grilling apparatus. Since he had the asparagus in the steamer, already topped with butter and pepper, all I had to do was turn on the stove.

We all sat down to eat salad—all of us, except for Scott. He was standing outside at the grill turning tuna kabobs. One of our guests asked that his tuna be "well done," so I went to the door to issue that request.

"They're almost done," Scott informed me. "Just check on the asparagus."

When I went into the kitchen, the asparagus smelled a little funny, but I figured that was pretty normal for asparagus. It looked a healthy bright green, so I used the tongs to put some on each plate, next to a scoop of Scott's fluffy basmati rice. Scott topped the rice with two kabobs, and I carried the first two plates into our guests. By the time I made it back to the dining room with my second pair of plates, one of our guests was holding a stick of asparagus like a pencil. "It's not cooked," he said.

"Gosh," I said. "It should be. It was in there a long time." Upon returning to the kitchen, I realized that I had "steamed" the asparagus over nothing but flame. Scott had prepped the steamer pot with everything needed for steaming, except the water. I suppose it was the second cocktail that had convinced me not to check that. The bottom of our new stainless steel pot was still glowing orange like a piece of iron at a blacksmith's forge.

I returned to the dining room, grabbed the asparagus off our laughing dinner guest's plates with tongs, ran back to the kitchen, threw it in another pot, and started re-steaming.

Meanwhile, back at the dining table, our four guests weren't yet sinking their teeth into Scott's tuna kabobs. "Don't wait on us," I insisted, pouring more wine. "Go ahead and eat."

"We can't," our friend admitted. "It's kinda raw."

I picked up my tuna kabob. It wasn't kinda raw. It was a chilly chunk of sushi ice. "Oh no," I cried. "Where's the shrimp?"

"I decided not to make that," Scott said, not yet realizing we were all aghast at his raw tuna. "I thought the tuna would be enough."

"Oh, it's enough alright," one friend laughed.

I choked on a gulp of red wine, and the rest of the table broke their polite silence and started laughing.

"I'm so glad you're the kind of friends we can be honest with," one of our friends said sweetly. "We love you guys."

"What should we do?" I choked hysterically.

"Have you ever heard of salt and pepper?" he asked.

"How about making a reservation?" another joked.

The way I see it, if laughter is the best medicine, it's bound to be good for dinner too. So is last minute takeout Chinese.

32

THE FUGITIVE

I can't remember what actually started the fight. I can only remember what ended it—a gun pointed at my head.

Scott and I had spent the day as we did many that summer, with Scott selling real estate, me writing on a deadline, and then driving together up to the country for some nighttime hours of painting, fixing, and arguing about colors, fabric, and where to put up or knock down walls. After a year, we were getting some serious work done at Edgewater Farm and having some powerful barks at each other in the process.

"Fine."

"Fine!"

We were silent in the car on the way to the house, silent when Scott dropped the keys in our dark driveway and spent five minutes searching for them, and even silent as we came inside the house and discovered that the carton of strawberries we had left on the counter had taken on a life of their own. Normally, Scott would have picked up the red hairy creature and chased me through the house with it. There was none of that fun on this night. In fact, "Fine."-"Fine!" were the last two words Scott and I had spoken to each other for three hours and that was *fine* with me.

I huffed while I washed my face. I exhaled noisily as I stripped and dramatically tossed my clothes on the floor. I stomped over to flick off the light and plodded back over to the bed. Downstairs, Scott was scurrying about in the living room like a rat in leaves, shuffling papers and pretending to still work.

I tossed to the left. I fluffed my pillow. I flipped to the right. I took a drink of water. I rubbed my feet together. I took a deep breath. Sigh-two-three-four-FINE-six. I tossed to the left. I refluffed my pillow. I took a deep breath. Sigh-two-three-four-finally-m-my-m-mind-began-to-to-float-and-drool-began-dripping-and-BAM! Jasper began howling. He leapt off the bed and stood at the floor to ceiling window in our bedroom, growling ferociously.

I sat up straight in bed. "DEER IN THE ROSES!" I yelled. Jasper's nails clicked across the hardwood floor, his bulky body hurtled down the stairs, and he barked viciously at the front door.

"Hey!" Scott suddenly yelled over Jasper's barking. "What the hell are you doing in my yard? Get out of here!"

Hell? I thought. *Scott never talks like that. Why is he cursing at the deer?* Suddenly, flashlights streamed through our house's windows like the scene in *E.T.* when the men in radioactive suits show up. I popped out of bed naked as the day I was born and ran for the stairs.

"Scott?" I hollered down the steps. "What's going on?"

Then, I heard the voice.

"Police!" a man's voice in our yard announced. "Come out of the house with your hands up!"

Scott walked onto the front porch, and from my bird's eye view down the stairs I could see him standing in his hip-high, tighty whities, illuminated by the beams of multiple flashlights. My thought was, *Wow, I never noticed that Scott looks like Antonio Sabato, Jr.* Why I wasn't thinking, *Oh my God, we're going to die!* I'm not sure.

"Who is in there with you?" the voice on the other side of the screen door asked.

"Bruce Littlefield," Scott announced, almost too willingly.

"Who?"

"My, uhm, partner."

"Can he come out?"

I walked down the stairs dazed and confused. "What's going on?" I asked, using my hands like a fig leaf in Eden. I stood at the screen door and peered out into the black night, grateful no one was saying, "hands up!"

"Do you mind if I grab a robe?" I asked.

"Sure," the voice said.

I quickly grabbed one from the closet and walked to stand with "Antonio" and Jasper on the front porch. Our house was surrounded by police. There were officers in the front, officers in the back, and officers in the perennials. They all had their hands on their guns.

"Keep your dog back!" someone instructed. "There's a police dog in the yard."

"What. Is. Going. On?" I asked for the third time, as Jasper desperately tried to get off the front porch and attack the figures lurking about our yard.

"I'm Officer So-and-So," one of them explained. "We have information that a fugitive may be staying in your house."

"A FUGUTIVE!" I yelped, looking back through the screen door, then whispering. "How do you know?"

An officer stepped onto the front porch and said point blank, "a reliable source."

"What kind of a 'reliable source?'" I asked.

"I'm not at liberty to reveal that information," the officer explained. "But it's a church lady." I looked at Scott standing in his skivvies and thought that one of our friend's had really pulled one over on us. We were on one of those *Jackass* shows or something. This had to be a practical joke.

"You mean, Dana Carvey?" I asked, playing along.

"Who?" the officer asked.

"The Church Lady?" I said, winking at him. *"Saturday Night Live."*

"No," he continued seriously. "The church up the road. This man may be armed and dangerous." I looked up the driveway. There were an awful lot of police cars up there.

"What'd this guy do?" Scott asked.

"He beat a police officer over the head with a baseball bat," one of them explained.

"Well, he's not here," Scott said firmly. "You're welcome to take a look around." A police officer stepped into our living room and scanned the area.

"Maybe, he's in the cottage." I volunteered. "Or how about next door at Don's? Don's not there."

"How do you know Don's not there?" the officer asked.

"He's dead."

"Yeah," Scott agreed with me for the first time that night. "The church lady probably meant over there."

"10-11s" "10-4s" and "7-11s" squawked on police radios in the background. In my robe, I offered to go with them to the property next-door "to just make sure."

"That won't be necessary," the detective said, as apparently another reliable source had just spotted the Fugitive up the road. "Sorry, gentlemen, for disturbing your night. If you ever need anything, don't hesitate to call us."

One after another, the police cars pulled out of our driveway, taking with them any memory of our earlier fight.

"Well, that was weird," I said. Then, I got right to the important question: "Do you think they saw my weiner?"

"Without a doubt," Scott laughed. "Without a doubt."

Little did we know that night, as we went around the house checking beneath beds and inside closets, that our cameo roles on C.O.P.S. were about to blossom into series regulars.

33

KNOCK KNOCK

The following week I opened the door to Edgewater and instantly knew that something was wrong. Jasper was nowhere in sight and there were smears of blood on the sofa. "Oh no," I said aloud.

It had, according to *Blue Stone* writer Jan Clyburn been "an odd summer in Stone Ridge"—it seemed that a fugitive had been running around, dodging police, and wreaking havoc on the four hours of sleep Scott and I were trying to get a night. As a courtesy to me, Jan didn't mention the police appearance at our house in her story, but everyone in town seemed to know about it anyway. A man stopped me at the farm stand. "You seen your friend?" he asked.

"Who?"

"Your friend."

"Who's that?"

"You know," he said, looking around furtively. "The fugitive."

"No," I said. I could tell he either thought I was hiding something, or worse, he'd heard that the police had seen my meat-n-potatoes. "Why?"

"I saw the helicopter," he said.

Later the same day, the cashier at the hardware store looked at me with concern in her eyes. "Is everything okay?" she asked.

"What do you mean?" I asked back.

"Oh," she said, "We just heard that there were a lot of cop cars at your house."

I was a boy hanging on the edge—finishing a book and zipping back-and-forth between city and country. Dealing with search teams in camouflage and low-flying helicopters somehow just made it all surreal. Now, there was blood on my sofa and my reality was so askew that my first thought was: *I wonder if my cleaning warranty is still in effect*. Well, that's what I wondered until I saw the blood on the loveseat, the disheveled pillows, and then the empty plastic bag on the floor.

"JASPER!" I screamed.

There wasn't a fugitive in the house there was a FOODgitive, and I heard his tail thumping on the kitchen floor—a sure-sign of dog gone wrong. "Jasper! What? Did. You. Do?!"

Since Jasper doesn't actually speak much, we've become quite proficient at translating his terribly sorrowful eyes and his perky tail: "*I didn't do it. And, if I did, I'm sorry*." Wag. Wag. "*Really sorry*." Wag. Wag. Wag. "*Really, really sorry*." Wag. Wag. Wag. (Pause.) "*You got a treat?*" Wag-Wag.

"You shouldn't have done that," I scolded, looking at his skinned nose. He had obviously cut it on the spiky points of the breadbasket he'd pulled off the kitchen counter.

"*I love you*," he said with a dramatic paw lift.

I leaned down to pet him and his tail suddenly sashayed faster than a Liberace metronome. "*That bread was good. Really good. Really really good.*" I grabbed a dishtowel and left Jasper distending in the kitchen. I was about to begin blotting the blood when I noticed a piece of bread wedged between the two back cushions. Pulling back the beige pillows revealed Jasper's diabolical scheme: he'd hidden hunks of bread in both the sofa and the loveseat for later.

The police had told us to look for signs of things missing, not for things buried in the couch. "Clothes, food, bikes, weapons," the Opie Taylor-looking officer had explained on one of the numerous follow-up visits he made to our house. "Do you have any guns?"

"Water guns," I had laughed. "A couple of water guns."

"Well, he may be armed," the officer reminded me seriously. "And he may be on bike." *Well, if he's on bike*, I thought, *why would he need one of ours?* I visualized the fugitive riding down our road on my Huffy from K-Mart with our neon water gun tucked in his belt. Then, I realized I had no idea what this guy looked like. The police had never told us, and I'd never thought to ask. Maybe they thought we were really hiding him, or perhaps they just let that small detail slip by.

"What's he look like?" I asked the officer on this particular visit.

"He's about five-ten," he explained.

"Uh huh," I nodded. "And?"

"And he's, um, dark skinned."

"What do you mean 'dark skinned?'" I asked.

"You know, like Indian."

"Indian?" I pried.

"Yes."

"Red dot or feather?"

"Feather."

"I see," I said, nodding. "Have you guys checked the house next door lately?"

"Yeah," he said. "Nothing."

Earlier in the week, the editor of the *Blue Stone* told me that she had noticed three tomatoes were missing from her garden. "They were almost ripe," she griped. "I was getting ready to pick them, and then they were gone."

"Oh, no," I empathized, knowing the grand expense of the three tomatoes we had grown that year. "What'd you do?"

"I called the police!" she said. "They said it was probably nothing. But it's just so weird. Have you noticed anything strange at your house?"

Oh, I thought, *you mean the unmarked cars, the helicopters, standing in front of a dozen cops naked, or the people in the basement at six in the morning?* "Nah," I said. "Nothing. But I told them I bet he's next door in Don's old house."

During the height of all the hullabaloo, Scott and I had decided to go over and take a look at the place next door. We were actually about to sign a contract to buy the property from Don's family and had waived the building inspection. We decided we should at least get a handle on what kind of project we were getting ourselves into.

As we walked down the long driveway, my heart raced. I grabbed Scott's arm and stopped him. "What if we run into the Fugitive?" I asked.

"Don't worry, Bruce," he said. "He's not here. The police have checked."

We walked toward the shack-like house, and as we got closer, we both stopped dead in our tracks. Something was definitely amiss. "There are sheets covering the windows and the doors are closed," I pointed. "Those doors have been open for months, and the windows have been curtainless!" I turned on my heels and began walking back. "Come on! Let's get out of here." *Zoinks*! A wanted criminal was living there! The Fugitive! I scurried back to Edgewater and breathlessly picked up the phone.

"9-1-1? I-know-where-the-fugitive-is," I panted. Suddenly, I was Gladys Kravitz from *Bewitched*, squealing that I had definitely seen Julius Caesar appear in my neighbor's kitchen right after she wiggled her nose. "No, he's not in my house. Yet. I mean, I haven't bought the house he's in, but I'm… I'm not really sure what kind of fugitive he is. But the police told me he may be armed."

The police were at the house in minutes. "Yes, he has been staying there," one officer confirmed. "But we've thrown all his clothes out in the yard, so he'll think twice before coming back."

It was all too much for me. "Why didn't they stake it out?" I asked Scott that afternoon as we drove out of the driveway. "If he knows they know…" A month of these antics on top of our usual antics was one set of antics too much. Then one night, the night of Jasper's bread hunt, it all came to a dramatic head.

Jasper and I were home alone when, a little after nine o'clock, there was a knock at the door. Curiously, Jasper didn't bark. I opened the door and saw an unfamiliar face on the other side of the screen door. "Are you Bruce?" the man asked.

"Yes. Who are you?"

"You know who I am."

"ARE YOU THE FUGITIVE?!" I yelped.

"Yep. That's me."

I suddenly realized why the police, looking through our windows had thought the Fugitive was in our house—he sort of looked like Scott. He was tall, dark, and handsome, with a cleft chin and a Hollywood smile. "They didn't tell me you were good looking," I said. He laughed.

I got right to the point. "Did you do it?" I asked.

"What's it?" he asked.

"Whatever it is," I said, "did you do it?"

"No."

"Then why are you running?"

"Cause they have it out for me."

"Who are 'they?'"

"The police."

"Were you in my basement early one morning a few weeks ago?"

"Nope," he told me through the screen door. "I've never been in your house."

I stepped onto the porch. "Well, did you take my editor's tomatoes?"

"Who?"

"The tomatoes from the stone house up the road."

"I haven't taken anything, man."

"Well then, I don't understand why you are running from the police."

"I don't want to go to jail. I don't want to miss the summer."

I was standing on my porch with a difficult burden. Here's a guy I'd never met before, a man who had caused me to live in fear, who had suddenly shown up and knocked on my door. Why me, I don't know. My heart was racing almost as fast as my mind. I knew that if I ran in to call the police, he'd be gone like a crow in the night. Or worse.

So I asked, "You want a beer?"

"Sure man," he said.

We sat down in my living room, and over a couple of Coronas, we had a very serious conversation. "You realize that they're going to eventually catch you," I said, noting my nervously parched tongue. "Or they'll just shoot you. Why don't you get a lawyer and turn yourself in? You can't always live on the lam."

"I don't like lawyers," he said.

"Look," I said pointblank. "Here's the deal. If you don't turn yourself in, you're going to get killed, and I can't live with that on my conscience. And, honestly, it's really not fair to put me in this position."

"Do you think I'm guilty?"

"It's not for me to decide," I said. "I'm not a judge or a jury. But I do think you have to understand that at some point in life you have to answer to authority."

"God is my authority," he said.

I smiled at him. "That's a good start," I said. "But we do live in a land where there are laws...." I paused. "I read the story in the paper, the interview with your parents. They obviously love you, and your neighbors spoke kindly of you. You don't want to do anything that's going to break their hearts."

We sat silent for a few moments, staring at each other. The crickets chirped and a gentle breeze blew down the creek and through the screen door.

"I'll turn myself in on Monday," he said.

"Is that a promise?" I asked.

"Yep."

"Take someone with you so you can do it peacefully," I suggested. He nodded. I gave him a hug, and, like a fleeting thought, he was gone.

The following Monday, as promised, the fugitive was a fugitive no more.

A *Blue Stone Press* article reported the event: "*Thirty-four-year-old Derrick Hardenburg turned himself over to State Police authorities at the barracks just south of Kingston Monday, ending a manhunt that began with a traffic stop on June 19. For more than a month, the peaceful hamlet of Stone Ridge had been turned upside down as state police helicopters, search dogs, and SWAT teams combed the woods repeatedly.*

Hardenburg, accused of speeding and of swinging a baseball bat inside his car when an officer approached it, has been described by neighbors and family as a basically harmless soul with a history of clashes with the powers that be, some of which resulted in his being abused and led him to react to uniformed officers in unfortunate ways.

All concerned hoped for a peaceful resolution.

That wish was granted when Hardenburg, his parents, and Blue Stone Press reporter Jan Clyburn arrived at the barracks to put an end to the manhunt."

And with the end of the manhunt for the neighborhood fugitive, our first year at Edgewater Farm came to a close.

34

THE GIFT

Whatever possessed (and possessed is the correct word) me to do it, I don't know. But I did. I decided to give in and get Scott a violin for our one-year anniversary in the house. I suppose my heart warmed at the thought of Scott's face lighting up like a kid getting his first bike. *Who am I to stymie creativity?* I asked myself. And, in one of my weaker moments on eBay, in one quick dissonant chord, I ordered a violin.

As the calendar counted down to its arrival, I found that my anticipation grew like that of a toothless six-year-old the night before Christmas. A delay notice from the seller began to give me second thoughts. *Should I take it as a sign to cancel?* As I waited for the UPS van to rumble down our driveway, the original buzz wore off. I envisioned signing for it and then secretly carrying it directly to the burn pile. The thought of screeching violin strings interrupting the peaceful sound of our babbling brook began playing on my auditory nerve.

When Scott's violin did finally arrive, *after* our anniversary, he happened to be standing right next to me. I smiled, almost genuinely, and handed it to him. "I can't believe it…" Scott said, as he tore into the tellingly shaped package. "I can't believe it!"

"I can't believe it myself!" I said, as he opened the case. We both gasped at the sight—a broken in half violin with sheep gut strings flapping in the breeze. "What do you say let's take this as a sign from God?" I asked. I firmly believe some things are meant to be and others just aren't. Who are we to question why? Scott shook his head.

I resealed the box and took it to the post office. Scott would get his violin come hell or high pitches. En route back, I stopped by the farm stand to pick up that week's copy of the newspaper.

Every week for a year, my column in the *Blue Stone* had sat opposite the obituaries. Early on, when I asked editrix Lisa Miller why, she explained, "I like to think of it as balanced reporting. Happy news on one page, sad news on the other."

"I get it," I told her. "I'm 'Moving In,' and they're 'Moving On.'"

An obituary in the paper caught my eye. Charlotte Hunt, the matriarch of Edgewater Farm, had died. I was sad, but my heart gladdened at a memory. A few months before, as spring was in full bloom, I decided that it would be nice to sit down with the grand dame of Edgewater and ask her to give me an oral history of the farm and bungalow colony. I called and asked if she had any time to talk.

Mrs. Hunt invited me over to her big ranch house on top of the hill. She said she wanted me to see her collection of memories from when she and husband Lansing ran the summer resort at what was now our house. Until that day, I had never actually met Mrs. Hunt, but Scott and I had felt her genuine spirit many times within the walls of our house.

"You drove over?" a sweet voice called out her backdoor as I got out of the Wagoneer. Mrs. Hunt's house is literally across the road.

"I thought maybe I'd drive you over to Edgewater later," I explained. "So you could see what we've done with the place."

"Oh, I don't know about that," she declared, shaking her head. "I haven't been back since we left in '64."

"*19*-64?" I asked as we walked into her house. "Mrs. Hunt, it's right across the street. You can see my front yard from your window."

Charlotte Hunt looked younger than the eighty-seven-year-old she claimed to be and moved faster than many half her age. As she gave me a tour around the ranch house her husband Lansing built, she darted about the rooms grabbing miscellaneous photos and Edgewater Farm memorabilia.

"Now, where are all those postcards?" she huffed, brushing aside a lock of hair that had sprung onto her forehead. "I know I put them right there." She pointed to the top of the organ sitting in her living room.

When we found them on the dining room table, she patted her blue short-sleeved dress and decided, "I guess my son was looking at them." Her lips, tinted the color of Scott's favorite rose, smiled a rather large smile for a small woman. "We all like to look at the memories from the farm. We had some really wonderful times there. It was an amazing time."

Mrs. Hunt and I sat down on the sofa and began to go through her collection of all things Edgewater. "Do you want some lemonade?" she asked as I became enveloped in the history of my house. I nodded, and she was up again. She brought in lemonade, cookies, and a stack of old brochures. "You're going to love these," she promised.

She handed me a tri-fold. I looked down at a picture of our house beneath the headline "Edgewater."

HUNT'S EDGEWATER FARM
R.D. 3 - Ulster County
KINGSTON, N.Y.
Phones: June 15 - Sept. 15 FE 1-6680
Off Season FE 1-5328

Memory Lane

Main Dining Room

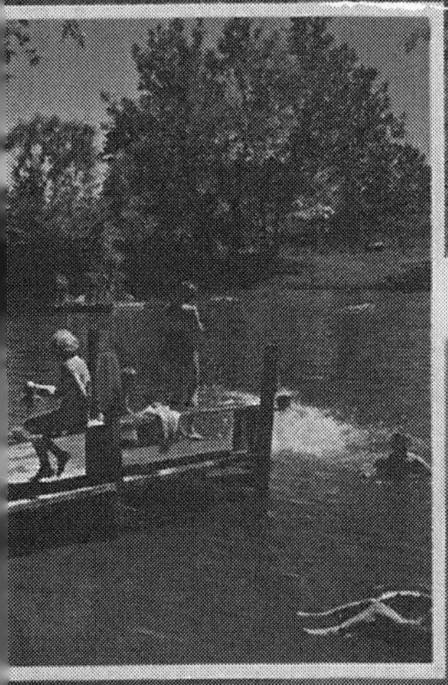

Springtime on The Farm

Ranch House Bedroom

The inside of the brochure heralded all things wonderful and promised potential guests that "the life of the farm is casual and gay."

"It still is, Mrs. Hunt!" I laughed.

"But can you get served a delicious breakfast, lunch, and dinner every day?" she challenged. "Plus sleep 'cottage cool' for only fifteen dollars a week?"

"Nope. We've tried at least one breakfast, lunch, and dinner—and they all didn't work out so well," I admitted. "And though I sleep 'cottage cool,' it'd be cooler if it were fifteen dollars a week."

"Edgewater is a place for relaxation and for living outdoors in the fresh air and sunshine," I continued reading. "It is a place where one may enjoy a few hours of fun with friendly folks or rest undisturbed.... An ideal spot for just the sort of vacation that you are probably seeking—where there is found freedom, and wide open spaces; where you can dress just as you wish to dress..."

I looked up at her and asked, "Have you seen me checking the mail in my Scooby Doo pajamas?"

"I've never even seen you until today," she admitted.

"Then, your write up is right, Mrs. Hunt," I said. "It is 'ideal for privacy.'"

After a couple hours of history, she gave me a gift—some old postcards, beautiful pictures, and a handful of the brochures. I wanted her to see the present Edgewater Farm. "Let's go over," I begged. "You can show me around."

"Oh, I'd like to," she said quietly. "But I shouldn't. My son will be home soon, and he'll wonder where I am."

"Here," I said, ripping a page from my notebook, "Leave him a note." And with that, I kidnapped Charlotte Hunt and drove her down her driveway and across the street to the house that she had called home for thirty years but had not visited in nearly forty. We rumbled down the driveway in the Wagoneer. "Sorry about that mess," I said, as we passed a pile of boards. "We're renovating the cottage."

"Oh, the Rec Hall?" she noted. "We used to have card games and parties and shows in there."

"Shows?" I said. "After we finish renovating it, I want to put on a show!"

"We have some tapes I can show you," she said.

I helped her out of the car and around the house. She stopped. "Wow!" she said. "You have a lot of flowers." Our delphiniums stood tall; our butterfly bushes bowed. The matriarch was home. Beneath her glasses, her eyes watered. "Mrs. Noble always did our flowers," Mrs. Hunt reminisced. "She'd be so proud."

"I'll tell Immy," I promised her.

Mrs. Hunt suddenly became as animated as a child in FAO Schwarz, pointing, remembering, and smiling. "That," she said, looking at our fountain, "was our well."

"I figured that out," I explained. "Given all the work it took someone to hand dig it, Scott and I decided that we didn't want to cover it up. So, we turned it into a fountain."

She nodded approvingly.

When we walked into the house, I watched a wave of memories wash over Charlotte Hunt's face like a summer rain. She pointed to what is now our living room and kitchen. "We served eighty people three meals a day in here all summer long for more than thirty years," she said. I decided not to mention that the current two occupants couldn't cook a can of beans.

I helped Mrs. Hunt climb the stairs, and we walked into our guest room.

"We nicknamed this room 'Butch,'" I told her.

"Butch? That's a funny name for a room!"

I pointed to the faded red trunk at the foot of the bed with the hand lettering on its side. "It's after that old camp trunk I found," I explained.

"This room is where my husband and I slept," she said, sighing a deep breath. Realizing it had been the master bedroom, I pretended I needed to go to the bathroom. I sat down on the toilet, put my face in my hands, and caught my emotions. In one short second, I had a tangible realization that the clock ticks and life changes, no matter how much we do to try and stop it. I thought of the Goethe quote: "Nothing is worth more than this day."

I collected myself and came out of the bathroom to find Mrs. Hunt quietly admiring the house. "What you've done here..." she said, "is *really* nice. Thank you for showing me."

I sent Mrs. Hunt flowers the next day and a note telling her how much we will always cherish the memories of our stay at Edgewater Farm. I wanted her to know.

After her death, I looked back at the old Edgewater Farm brochure once again. A line caught my eye: "...And you may be sure that, once discovered, Edgewater is not easily forgotten."

EDGEWATER FARM, R.D. 1, KINGSTON, N. Y.

THE HOMESTEAD, EDGEWATER FARM, R. D. 1, KINGSTON, N. Y.

RECREATION HALL, EDGEWATER FARM, KINGSTON, N. Y.

"THE SHALLOWS" EDGEWATER FARM, R.D. 1, KINGSTON, N.

There is a Tibetan ritual of making sand paintings with millions of grains of colored sand painstakingly laid into place on a flat platform. The process takes weeks, and the result is an unbelievably intricate and exquisite painting. When finished, to symbolize the impermanence of all that exists, the colored sands are swept up and poured into a nearby river where the waters carry the healing energies throughout the world.

We'd had our first year at Edgewater Farm and already enjoyed a thousand memories. Mrs. Hunt's death reminded me that one day we too will move out, and some other lucky people will be moving in. My prayer is that they will cherish the gift the way we do.

AFTERWORD (LOOKING FORWARD)

The day that gay marriage was legalized in New York, our cell phones came alive. Friends and loved ones wanted to know if Scott and I had set the date. Many also requested to be apprised of their titles and roles at the wedding. Deb, Scott's ex-girlfriend who introduced us, asked for and was promised the role of Flower Girl. My brother announced that he would like to be the one to give me away.

There was only one problem with all of that—we currently have no plans to get married. We like what we have. Even though it's unlicensed, unsanctioned, and at times unbelievable, it's just between us. And, on most days, if Scott's not driving, it works.

Trust me, we're committed. I just suppose that after twenty years of togetherness, neither of us has felt the urge to add a "salad spinner" to our gift registry at Bed, Bath and Beyond.

However, let it be said that we both firmly and heartily believe it should be everyone's right to get married to whomever they love, but that no two people should *have* to in order to prove their love and commitment. I appreciate that marriage is a great institution; I'm just not sure I'm ready to be institutionalized.

Even though we don't have a piece of paper or a wedding registry, we're a couple—a couple of what, exactly, might still be questionable. We disagree on paint; we argue about money; and one of us never remembers birthdays, while the other one never forgets them. Depending on the topic, it's a 50/50, 60/40, 30/70 relationship. One of us, for example, tolerates the other rearranging the furniture in the middle of the night, obsessing over Christmas, and ordering way too much off eBay, while the other tolerates bad driving, penny pinching, and occasional gassiness.

If you've ever been in a relationship, ours probably seems very familiar. Yes, we may be a gay couple, but our life really isn't that different. Our lawn still needs to be cut, just like yours. Our dog barks, eats and poops, just like yours. And our washing machine breaks the week after the warranty expires, just like yours.

In fact, except for the prejudices we face (and that we can both use the same public bathroom), a "gay" relationship isn't really all that different than a "straight" relationship. Why? As any heart will tell you: love is love is love.

Celebrating our 20th Anniversary in Santorini, Greece.

The day that gay marriage was legalized in New York was the same day that Scott wrecked both our cars, simultaneously. Yep, he backed up the driveway during a sneezing fit and slammed the SUV into the tailgate of the truck. I didn't bat an eye. Had the accident been an out of the ordinary incident in our twenty-year narrative, I may have responded with alarm, shock, or anger. Instead, after the impact and its jolting lurch forward, I sat remarkably stoic, diligently writing my "To Do" list on the back of a piece of junk mail while he got out to inspect the damage.

"Well?" I asked, as he climbed back into the driver's seat.

"There's damage," he said without looking at me.

As we drove up the driveway, I added "Call Toyota" to my "To Do" list... right after, "Pick new paint color for the house" and right before, "Ask Scott to marry me."

ACKNOWLEDGMENTS

Our story would never have happened without the wonderful Deb Drucker. What other angel on earth could have a big enough heart to spend months helping her boyfriend, whom she considered marriage material, come out of the closet, only to then set him up with her male friend… me? She's one of a kind.

I'm ever grateful for the readers of the *Blue Stone Press* and publisher Lori Childers, who, for six years, let me tell the tales of two guys buying a place in the country. The *Blue Stone Press* is a Hudson Valley treasure.

I'm thankful to ABC *Shark Tank* star Barbara Corcoran for your friendship, your inspiration, and for your great job editing this book!

I'm grateful to Rita Cosby, Lis Wiehl, Zach Wahls, Elisabeth Hasselbeck, Daniella Cracknell, Dianne Chinnes, Todd Shuster, Chase Bodine, Shelley Lewis, Sarah LaDuke, Jill Capuzzo, JL Stermer, Al Vaz, Colleen McCarthy, Scott Durkin, Marta

Schooler, Gretchen Crary, Eric Brown, Barb Frederick, and the legendary Sy Presten who have all played a vital role in some part of my career. I'm ever appreciative to publishers Random House, Grand Central, Harper Collins, Simon & Schuster, Wiley, and Penguin Putnam for allowing me the opportunity to do great projects.

Cheers to Kathy McKinney Brewer, my hometown valedictorian, for sharing her smart thoughts on this book and to my editorial assistants Karina Grudnikov and Jessica Toomer for constantly coming through. Thanks to artist Paul Heath for always sharing his artistic talents with my projects and for creating the Moving In logo. An extra burpee for my trainer Greg Gomez and a big hug for Mercedes Sanabrea who helps keep me (and our house!) together.

I am indebted to all our neighbors in the Catskills who befriended us, taught us everything from gardening to sump pumps, and made us feel loved and equal. You all know who you are, even though to protect the innocent I cleverly changed your names.

To the memory of our beloved Jasper and to our wonderful Westminster, thank you for the unconditional love and the fantastic fun.

And finally, to Scott—my friend, my partner, my love—thank you for putting up with me.